FIFTEENTH-CENTURY ENGLISH DRAMA

Fifteenth-century English Drama

The Early Moral Plays and their Literary Relations

W. A. DAVENPORT

D. S. BREWER · ROWMAN & LITTLEFIELD

© W. A. Davenport 1982

Published by D. S. Brewer
240 Hills Road, Cambridge
an imprint of Boydell & Brewer Ltd
PO Box 9, Woodbridge, Suffolk IP12 3DF

and in the United States
by Rowman and Littlefield
81 Adams Drive
Totowa, New Jersey 07512

British Library Cataloguing in Publication Data

Davenport, W. A.
    Fifteenth-century English drama: the early
    moral plays and their literary relations.
    1. Moralities, English
    I. Title
    822'.0516   PR643.M7

    ISBN 0-85991-091-1

Library of Congress Cataloging in Publication Data

Davenport, W. A. (William Anthony), 1935–
    Fifteenth-century English drama.

    I. Moralities, English—History and
criticism.   2. English drama—To 1500—History
and criticism.   I. Title.   II. Title: 15th
century English drama.
PR643.M7D3   1982   822'.0516'09   82-3665
ISBN 0-8476-7120-8   AACR2

Photoset in Great Britain by
Rowland Phototypesetting Limited, Bury St Edmunds, Suffolk
and printed by St Edmundsbury Press
Bury St Edmunds, Suffolk

Preface

My aim in this book has been to write a simple account of the different types of drama being written in fifteenth-century England. Particularly in need of re-assessment are the plays which are usually straitjacketed together under the heading 'morality plays'. I have combined appreciations of the four earliest English examples of allegorical drama with briefer discussions of other plays, some well-known, some rarely read, in the hope that the reader will share with me both the sense that early plays are more varied than is often suggested, and the realisation that medieval plays do not represent archaic dramatic forms looming like the skeletons of dinosaurs from a dead didactic past, but are simply early versions of familiar theatrical genres.

As a teacher concerned with medieval drama over a period of years, I have been aware of how difficult it is to find a satisfactory way of presenting the subject to beginners. In order to get a grip on diffuse and uncertain material and to introduce students in a limited time to large and partly over-lapping texts, the teacher has to generalise, condense and over-simplify, and to make classification too clear-cut. One is painfully reminded of the bad effects of doing all these things, when students either read far too little and think that the *Towneley Second Shepherds' Play* and *Everyman* are typical of the whole, or learn up dubious, second-hand literary history tracing the supposed growth of guild-plays from Latin tropes. This book is an attempt to lead on from a first acquaintance with the medieval drama to a wider exploration of fifteenth-century plays, especially the moralities, and of the connecting links between plays and among writings of the period in general.

The material is mainly familiar and I claim no originality or discovery; my direct debts to other scholars I have acknowledged wherever I am conscious of them, either in the text or in the notes. I have attempted to bring together ideas from a variety of sources and to re-assess them, to some extent, in the hope that the picture of medieval drama will look a little different as a result. I have assumed that the reader has a general knowledge of the mystery plays, *Everyman* and a few others, but have tried to keep in mind the needs of the general reader whose acquaintance with medieval literature is not extensive. Quotations from the plays follow, in the main, the editions cited in the Bibliography, but I have modernised the texts to the extent of eliminating obsolete letters and modifying the usage of i/j and u/v to conform to modern practice. I have, however, retained the visually odd spellings such as *xall* for 'shall' which are characteristic of the written dialect of East Anglia in the period.

I have been aided in my work on this book by the grant of a term's sabbatical leave by the Council and Principal of Royal Holloway College. I am grateful to Kay Thompson for typing part of the manuscript. My wife typed much of the rest, for which I am also grateful; grateful is too small a word to express my sense of all the other help and support she has given me.

Contents

CHAPTER ONE

Genres

1. Introduction

In many people's minds, I suspect, there is a fairly clear picture of Elizabethan drama being written by a carelessly elegant, dark-bearded man in a velvet doublet, sitting scribbling on a trestle-table in a tavern, with pots of sack and ink side-by-side and a boy dashing in with frantic messages from the nearby theatre. In contrast one has a vague idea that medieval drama was not written at all but somehow happened on the back of a cart in a communal mêlée of prosperous burgesses, rude mechanicals and pedantic clerics, compromising between the values of pit and pulpit. Even when one corrects the looseness of such impressions with factual historical detail, there remains a sense of the difference between plays which we can identify as written by individuals for particular theatres and audiences and the earlier blur of mainly anonymous, religious dramatic work, which has to be studied more as an aspect of social growth in the north and the east midlands than as literature.

In the past, medieval English drama was seen as part of a process of evolution. Ninth-century Latin choral chants, in which priests re-enacted the visitation of the three Maries to the tomb of Christ, were said to have grown into twelfth-century liturgical dramas, in which choirs performed elaborate dramatic celebrations of the key sacraments of the Christian year. These somehow (one never quite knew how) became a lot of short scriptural pageants in English, acted by honest medieval workmen, organised into guilds and expressing with simple faith the corporate Christian spirit of the Middle Ages. These in turn grew an appendix called moral interludes, before getting more and more comic and secular and turning into Elizabethan drama. This family tree always looked phoney and it is a relief to be able to discard it and to accept the more plausible modern view that the English mystery cycles were created by educated, literary men in the late fourteenth and early fifteenth centuries out of a combination of existing traditions of drama and religious material in sermons, instruction-books, scriptural summaries and paraphrases, commentaries and lyrics. The cycles are not so much part of a process of natural growth as a response, during a period of increasing literary activity in English, to a particular idea of celebration and entertainment: this was the idea of a civic and ecclesiastical marking of either the feast of Corpus Christi or Whitsuntide by a large-scale amateur performance of a professionally-written and professionally-organised text, which told the

Christian story, from the Creation of the World to the Last Judgment, in a series of short tableaux with dialogue.[1]

Other forms of drama in England were contemporary with the development of the cycles, rather than an off-shoot from them, and reflect the needs of different audiences and venues. During the fifteenth century, single plays, as opposed to cycles, were being composed to be performed in both public and private places, by both amateur and professional actors. Some were university plays; some were for great houses; some were popular. They (or at least the ones that have survived) were mainly didactic dramas; the principal type was the allegorical moral play. They were acted in one place (rather than in a series of 'stations' at which movable pageants halted), and so, whether the place was great hall or inn-yard, shared the dramatic possibilities provided by 'place-and-scaffold' staging.[2] Unlike the cycles, which were designed for annual performance and therefore revised at intervals, these plays were non-recurrent; some probably had a very limited theatrical life because of topical and local allusions.[3]

The idea of an unfolding of successive dramatic developments has, because of such differences, now been replaced by a new generalisation which separates medieval plays into different genres. With Latin liturgical dramas in one compartment, the surviving versions of the Corpus Christi cycle known as Chester, York, Towneley and the N-Town cycle (or, as it used to be called, *Ludus Coventriae*)[4], together with various separate pageants thought to have been once part of cycles, can go into another labelled 'mystery play' and be discussed as a single play with internal variations, since they had a common public purpose and were basically similar in material and pattern. Into other pigeon-holes go the rest of the plays surviving from the fifteenth and early sixteenth centuries, with the labels 'morality play' and 'saint's play' upon them. Under the heading 'morality play' come *The Pride of Life*, the three Macro Plays (*The Castle of Perseverance, Mankind* and *Wisdom*), *Everyman, Mundus et Infans, Hick Scorner, Youth*, and two plays by known authors, Henry Medwall's *Nature* and John Skelton's *Magnificence*. The 'saint's plays' are *The Conversion of St Paul* and *Mary Magdalene*, found in MS Digby 133 and known, together with *Herod's Killing of the Children* and another (incomplete) copy of *Wisdom*, as 'the Digby Plays'. Add to these some fragments and a few 'miscellaneous' plays, which don't fit into the categories (*Dux Moraud*, the Croxton *Play of the Sacrament, Christ's Burial and Resurrection*, Thomas Chaundler's Latin play, the *Liber Apologeticus*, and Medwall's *Fulgens and Lucrece*) and we have the range of extant medieval plays produced in England between the end of the fourteenth century and about 1520.[5]

The classifications are useful to the teacher and literary historian, but they have a number of drawbacks. They make one look at kinds of drama rather than plays, so that individual works tend to be seen as versions of an archetype rather than as achieving effects in their own right. There is also a natural desire to make the categories account for as many plays as possible, which leads to a glossing over of differences. Placed with the Chester, York and Towneley cycles, the N-Town cycle is a cuckoo in the nest; its differences from the other three are repeatedly more interesting than its similarities to them. The categories of mystery cycles, morality plays and so on have discouraged general interest in medieval drama; the phrases, especially 'morality play', sound boring and create the impression of a collection of dull, identical plays. In fact, if one looks at the complete collection of medieval plays, which I listed above, one is struck by the variety of dramatic ideas within them. (One is struck also by the large number of them which came from East Anglia or nearby areas.[6])

In this book I intend to explore the variety. What interests me particularly is the range of ideas within the plays known as 'morality plays', as well as the currents which run between the plays in different categories. The moral plays and the cycles have many things in common: the N-Town cycle is a combination of the two. Each of the plays is an individual treatment of ideas, and there are many differences of scope, style and stage effect even when themes are shared. With the moral plays there is evidence within the drama of the different theatres and audiences for which they were written, and enough signs of methods of performance for one to know that techniques of theatre in the fifteenth century were varied and sophisticated. However, theatre history has been given more attention than the actual content of medieval drama, and I prefer to emphasise the composition of these plays. Their nature is best understood, I believe, from a literary point of view, not from a theatrical, although stage-craft is obviously one of the literary skills necessary for the creation of a good dramatic text.

In each of the four chapters that follow this one I intend to take one moral play as starting-point. I will examine the play itself and try to show what is creative, imaginative and individual about it and then try to show its relationship to other plays which share its ideas and qualities. I have chosen the four earliest moral plays because they are the foundations of one's sense of the supposed 'genre', the morality play, and because their differences from one another show what an unstable category 'morality play' is. The earliest of them is the incomplete *The Pride of Life*, a number of scenes based on the theme of the vanity of earthly power in the face of death, probably written in the late fourteenth century; it is a suitable starting-point for a consideration of medieval tragedy. The three earliest complete allegorical plays in English are the Macro Plays. These three East Anglian works were written at different times in the fifteenth century and were later joined together in one manuscript, from whose eighteenth-century owner, an antiquarian clergyman from Bury St Edmunds named Cox Macro, they take their group title. Among them the three plays express a broad range of dramatic aims and interests. *Mankind* is the most scurrilous of medieval plays and includes so much mockery of virtue and knockabout farce that it was, in the past, usually described as a degenerate play, which showed the homiletic drama in danger of falling into secular decadence for the sake of pleasing a popular audience; it represents some, at least, of the medieval idea of comedy. *Wisdom* is a complex mixture of spectacular costumes, dances and abstract ideas; human nature is present in the three aspects of Mind, Will and Understanding; it sets one thinking about the cerebral and formal aspects of drama and the later masque. *The Castle of Perseverance* is the earliest of the three and the most elaborate both in staging and content; the sketch in the manuscript of its circular acting area and scaffolds is centrally important to historians of the medieval theatre; its combination of all the main themes of the moral plays – the corruption of human nature by the World, the Flesh and the Devil, the battle between the Seven Deadly Sins and the Seven Cardinal Virtues, the debate of the four daughters of God, the coming of death – make it one of the longest (and, one must admit, in places the most tedious) of medieval plays; it represents a different idea of drama from the others, a large-scale, panoramic and epic experience. In my last chapter I will return to a more general view. I hope that by then the pigeon-holes ('morality plays', 'mystery cycles', etc.) will have become inadequate as a filing-system. It is meet, however, that before discarding the system one should check on its advantages and disadvantages.

2. *Subject-matter, characters and form in the cycles and the moral plays.*

There are three main areas where one might argue that the separation of medieval plays into cycles on the one hand and morality plays on the other is necessary: these are the range and nature of the subject-matter, the nature of the speaking figures and the form of the plays.

The subject-matter of the cycles is historical. The pageants cover both the literal history, as recounted in Scripture and related early narratives, of specific events, people and times, and also the interpretation of history through Christian faith. So myth and prophecy join the chronicle of ancient times, as they do in the Bible, to form a complete account of life from the Creation of the World to the Last Judgment of men. The subject-matter of morality plays is limited in time to the present-day and to the span of an individual human life, from birth to death and the possible or actual salvation of the soul.

The characters who appear in the cycles are of two kinds: supernatural (God and his angels, from whom came the Devil and his demons, and Christ), and natural (individual human figures from Scripture, anonymous representatives of the people and a few commentators). The central figure of the cycles is Christ. In the morality plays the central figure is Man, but, despite this, there are no 'natural' characters: all the figures are either supernatural or figurative. The supernatural figures, God, Christ, Satan, etc., may or may not appear; ideas of good and evil may instead (or in addition) be represented by allegorical personifications of virtues and sins. Human beings are represented both by a personification of human nature (called Mankind, Everyman, etc.) and by the personification of aspects of human physiology and psychology (called Health, Reason, etc.).

The form of the cycles is episodic and panoramic. The short pageants are complete in themselves, but they depend for their logic on what precedes and follows: on the other hand, the contents of the cycle could vary, from year to year, without the essential idea of the 'play' being harmed. The pieces of the mosaic are organised by an over-all simple structural design, consisting of beginning (Creation and Fall), middle (Incarnation) and end (Redemption and Judgment). The form of the morality plays is not so easily defined, since they vary in length and scope, but all the moral plays are tauter in structure than the cycles: they are designed as a single (or, as in *Nature*, a double) shape, often with a strong sense of symmetry reflecting the theme. The pattern is basically that of innocence, corruption and repentance (or perhaps ignorance, experience and realisation would be better since that could embrace even *Everyman*); the succession of scenes is dictated not so much by chronological sequence (as it is necessarily with the historical material of the cycles) as by cause and effect.

So far, so good, if what one wants is a tidy list of characteristics, arranged in two columns, which will give one a sense that medieval drama has been classified, labelled and therefore understood. But so far, too simple, if one is honest. In each of the three areas of subject-matter, character and form, once one thinks beyond the obvious differences, qualifications occur. I will take the three areas one at a time.

SUBJECT-MATTER

In the cycles, though the subject-matter is historical, the point of reference in the treatment of the matter is often that of the life of the individual Christian here and now. The playwrights are concerned to show the working-out of the scheme of redemption, and they are often particularly inventive in scenes where the ordinary human reaction to great events can be expressed. In a sense, one can see a composite representation of mankind developing in the cycles from individual examples (from Adam, through Cain and Noah, to Lazarus, Thomas, and so on) and spreading out into the nameless figures of shepherds, torturers, and the examples of wisdom and folly divided on Judgment Day. The characteristic medieval use of anachronism encourages the audience to see events as happening in the present day. The realistic details which are put in for the sake of liveliness also bring the characters close to home. The result is that in the cycles, which are supposedly about the distant past, one finds a richer rendering of actual medieval living than in the supposedly 'contemporary' moral plays.

The moral plays do not dramatise Christian history, but they do not ignore it. They summarise it in the speeches of divine or virtuous characters, and they introduce into the plays homiletic reminders of Redemption and Judgment. The ideas of God's generosity to man, man's ingratitude and failure and his need to find in Christ's sacrifice the stimulus to repentance are the theoretical basis of the moral plays.

The cycles and the morality plays are two alternative ways of dealing with the same material, which is the Christian view of history and life on earth. One way is through scripture and historical figures. In the cycles literal histories are vividly recounted and the figures become types of human nature; the birth, death and resurrection of Christ are presented as factual chronicle for the audience's instruction and meditation. The other way is through intellectual analysis of the forces at work in man's own nature and in the normal span of life, so that the Christian scheme of redemption is re-enacted through the pattern of a man's life, which becomes a microcosm of the larger history of mankind. Again there is a sense that the audience is being asked to make Christian teaching meaningful in their own lives, helped by recognition, from what the play shows, of the pattern of existence.

The relationship between the two ways is akin to the relationship between medieval lyrics on the Passion and mortality lyrics. One offers realisation through Christ's suffering for man, the other through recognition of human weakness. But there is a point where the two types of lyric meet, in the sense that Christ shared man's flesh and frailty, and that his human body on the Cross is the most powerful image of mortality and reminder of the separability of flesh and spirit. So with the plays. They meet and over-lap in common themes and aims. Into the Scriptural material of the cycles are woven themes which elsewhere become morality plays: in the dramatisations of the fall of Lucifer, the temptation of Eve, the killing of Abel, and so on, the medieval playwrights use the same kind of words, speeches and stage effects as are found in allegorical scenes of pride and fall, weakness succumbing to flattery, envy destroying good, etc. Repeatedly one finds the conflict between good and evil, the illustration of sin and repentance, the examination and judgment of conduct. The central actions of the cycles are the events leading to the Crucifixion; these are dealt with in trial scenes and crowd scenes in which the inadequacies of men are exposed. The central scenes in the morality plays are often those of the temptation of man and his life in sin; this is where all the anguish and the fun tend to be, while homily and sanctity provide the material for the beginning and the end. Both plays thrive on the illustration of evil.

CHARACTER

To describe the cycles and the morality plays as essentially different because the characters in one are allegorical and in the other not seems to me misleading. There is much in common between the characters in the different types of play, despite the difference in what they are called.

In the case of supernatural figures, there is no distinction between cycles and moral plays, except in the variety of role in different parts of Christian history. God and His angels and Satan and his demons appear in the morality plays as rivals for the soul of man. In the presentation of this conflict the playwrights take up themes which occur in the cycles in the scenes of the temptation of Adam and Eve, the temptation of Christ, the debate of the Daughters of God, the Harrowing of Hell and the Last Judgment, as well as being implicit elsewhere. These are the main episodes in the cycles where supernatural powers, especially devils, appear: others deal with the Fall of the Angels, and the dream of Pilate's wife. In these scenes there is the same range in the demonic role as in the moral plays: it varies from overweening pride (leading to bellowing lamentation at the agony of punishment) to malicious plotting against God and man (manifesting itself in temptation, lying intrigue and confidential speech with the audience) and to the development of the demon into a satirical device through which man's folly and vice may be revealed. Significant points of comparison may be found in the Devil's Prologue to the Passion Play in the N-Town cycle and in the speeches of Tutivillus, who appears in both the Towneley *Judgement* play and in the moral play *Mankind*. In Continental plays the tradition developed of Satan as active participant in the events leading up to the Crucifixion, (as the tempter of Judas, present at the foot of the Cross, etc.) and there are some signs of knowledge of this tradition in the N-Town cycle. This increases the aspect of intrigue and rivalry in the treatment of the trials and death of Christ, and makes Satan's role very like that of the tempter in the moral plays.

With the human figures there is not such a complete identification of role between different types of play, but they do overlap. Many of the named historical figures in the cycles are presented simply as 'tableau' figures and given the speeches necessary for them to fulfil their function in unfolding the story. But some figures were far more developed and the main method of development was to use historical instances as exemplification of moral ideas. This is one main way in which the bare material of Scripture was expanded, so that in the individual example one saw the types of mankind. Hence Herod becomes the type of the ranting tyrant, boasting of worldly power, and brought down as punishment for pride; Pilate becomes a more complex version of the holder of power, because he holds in trust worldly justice as well as worldly command. Caiaphas and Annas become the occasion for the examination of judges and law-courts and the corruptions of office. Even more clearly the figures of the Old Testament appear in representative roles and in Adam, Eve and Cain we see the types of human weakness and evil, as in Noah, Abraham and Moses the types of virtue and faith. Even figures who were not so clearly exemplary are treated in ways which bring them close to the concerns of the morality playwrights: so the idea of the conflict within the mind between contrary impulses, towards faith and doubt, or towards right and wrong, interests the cycle dramatists just as much, and leads to extensive treatment of the doubts of Joseph, the succumbing to temptation and remorse of Judas, the uncertainty of Pilate.

The anonymous figures of soldiers, priests, lawyers, mothers, midwives, shepherds and so on show an even clearer tendency towards allegory. Even when their roles are simple and functional, the use of groups of two or three encourages the idea that they are a representative sample of human suffering, cruelty, innocence or guilt; the confrontation between the brutal soldiers and the protesting mothers in the pageants of the massacre of the innocents provides a good instance. Sometimes the effect created through these groups of anonymous figures is that of ritualising the action on stage, by means of symmetrical arrangement of speeches and/or actions, as when the three sons and daughters-in-law of Noah plead with their mother or help the building and stocking of the Ark, or when the three shepherds praise the Christ-child in turn. Even more striking is the scene in York Play XXV when eight burgesses greet Christ on his entry into Jerusalem with a stanza in turn, and bring the pageant to a close in a circle of acclamation of Christ, successively in all his aspects, moving from prophet, flower and blissful babe to conqueror, gleaming sun and judge.

Some of the minor figures achieved a traditional role, such as the doubting and believing midwives, the thieves at the Crucifixion, and the figure of the Janitor (whose role is imaginatively exploited by the creator of the York scene where Judas is confronted by the discerning Porter at the gate of Pilate's court). These roles are allegorical in cast, since they represent a move not towards portrayal of human individuality, but towards the expression of moral states or aspects of the mind and will. At times such figures identify themselves in an allegorical way, as do the Detractors in the *Trial of Joseph and Mary* in the N-Town cycle, where the pageant becomes an opposition between evil and innocence, in the manner of a moral play, as the two figures who slander Mary are identified as 'Raise-slander' and 'Backbiter'.

Finally, there are some clearly allegorical characters in the cycles. The main examples are the chorus figures, who appear under such names as Doctor, Expositor, etc.; they act as explicators of doctrine or to bridge the gap between Old and New Testaments. A good instance is found in Play XII in the York Cycle, where the Prologue is given a speech of 144 lines to explain man's loss of Paradise and the idea of the Incarnation and then to go through all the traditional prophecies of the coming of Christ, before the pageant deals, in only 96 further lines, with the Annunciation and the visit to Elizabeth. The role of such figures is close to that of the main homiletic personifications in a moral play. Occasionally the allegorical personae are developed and become not only commentators but characters in the action; this happens several times in the N-Town cycle, notably with Contemplacio in the Prologue to the *Salutation and Conception* and Mors in *The Death of Herod*. (I will discuss these more fully later.) With these roles the playwrights go outside the idea of simply bringing Scriptural material to theatrical life; they are commenting on, interpreting and judging the value of their material and employing non-historical characters to represent the Church or to personify forces which act within or upon man.

When one moves from the persons in the cycles back to those in the moral plays, one finds that the mixture is not as different as one expects. As I said earlier, the figures of God, Christ and the Devil are essentially the same. The rest of the characters may be personifications, but they are often treated in such a way as to make them typical of realistic human behaviour. This is particularly so with the evil and vicious characters and with the Mankind figure while he is leading a life of sin. So, while the Scriptural characters in the cycles tend to be assimilated into standard, exemplificatory patterns and to be treated in a generic, allegorising manner, the personifications in the moral plays tend to be presented as lifelike (as is clear when the plays are acted and one forgets their names) at least in some aspects of their being. The result is that the impression made by the figures in the two types of play is often the same; only the names are different. In both kinds of play the characters are used as mirrors of fifteenth-century society and as mouthpieces for the playwright's comments upon it; they are animated by the same energy of social satire. In both kinds of play the understanding of behaviour is based on Christian teaching in sermons, instruction books, allegorical tracts, religious lyrics, and so on, and there is a thin dividing line between the sort of non-allegorical teaching found in, say, the *Ancrene Wisse*, with its many instances of everyday sinful behaviour, and an allegorical analysis of the Seven Deadly Sins such as is found in *Piers Plowman*, in which under the names of personifications, the same traits of behaviour are exposed and condemned.

FORM

In neither cycles nor moral plays is there any strict sense of form. So, although there is a theoretical distinction between a play consisting of a series of short playlets and one complete in itself, in practice the distinction is less clear. The longer cycle pageants become short plays in their own right, with several scenes and a movement from exposition, through confrontation to resolution. The dramatic structure is not very different from that in the short moral play. Conversely the long moral plays consist of a large number of scenes, use a large cast and have a scope of theme comparable with the cycles. There are within the cycles also several features which make the structure seem accidental rather than an essential aspect of the play's meaning. There is, on the one hand, a sense of poor structure, of undigested lumps (especially of didactic matter such as the Prophecies of the coming of Christ) and confused intentions. On the other, there are examples of prior literary arrangements surviving into the cycles from collections of sermons or earlier plays: this is particularly true of the N-Town cycle where the Passion Plays are detachable from the cycle and where a group of plays about the Virgin Mary has been drawn on as a source.

Both cycles and moral plays are, of course, examples of verse-drama and in their use of verse one can find other bases for grouping plays together. The distinctions in the use of poetry are not between types of play, but between the places where, the times when, and the audiences for which the dramas were composed. East of the Pennines poetic style seems to have been more venturesome and flamboyant than is evidenced in the rather flat consistency of the Chester Cycle. In the earlier fifteenth-century East Midland plays (the York and Towneley plays and *The Castle of Perseverance*) there are attempts both at high style and at tougher, terser expression, which can be colloquial; the main decorative device is alliteration, which sometimes results only in a fussy, encumbered effect, but which can be dignified and resonant. The Wakefield Master's pageants in the Towneley Cycle favour a complex 9-line stanza, which one would think unsuited to dialogue, but which the playwright handles well enough to create a virtuoso flourish here and there (in the insults Noah and his wife hurl at one another, for instance). In the later fifteenth-century plays one can distinguish an East Anglian style, which has been influenced by the poetry of Lydgate. The style is marked by a liking for aureation (in Latinate vocabulary, that is), polysyllables, patterning and much repetition. At its worst such poetry is insufferably pretentious, but aureate style may be used in discriminating ways with particular dramatic purposes. In several plays the poets vary their metres for dramatic ends, and the very awareness of style which such variation indicates is something to which the reader responds. Into the plays a number of poetic forms were absorbed and one could produce a very readable anthology of medieval lyrics from the drama. At least one play *(Christ's Burial and Resurrection)* may appropriately be seen as a series of poetic complaints or laments. There was some idea of 'poetic drama' in the period, not just plays written in verse.

All I wish to suggest, for the moment, is that in both the cycle plays and the moral plays (and in the saint's plays and the rest), one finds evidence of interest on the part of the dramatists in form and style which is not peculiar to a particular kind of play. In all kinds the writers needed to express Christian teaching and the impression of holy sanctity and authority, and for these purposes they sought elevated diction and rhetorical patterns. On the other hand they were dealing with evil and

with everyday conduct and they needed expression which was pungent-
ly true to the tang of sin. One finds, similarly, a dependence in all types of
play of the period on certain formal devices: the long speech in which a
character defines his own nature, the inert homiletic commentaries, the
exclamatory scurrility of demons and so on. In the form of the plays as a
whole there is much uncertainty and variation, but also some evidence of
seeking a tauter structure (leading towards the eventual division of a play
into acts) and an interest in using style to express states of moral being.

3.   *Plays and other Middle English literature*

If one thing to be argued in favour of a broader approach to medieval
plays is that types of play have been kept in separate compartments and
their similarities forgotten, another is that use of the whole category
'medieval drama' has been a means of separating plays from other forms
of contemporary literature and thereby loosening the connections. Writers on medieval drama have often been interested only in the history of
the theatre, or have approached the subject backwards in a search for the
origins of Elizabethan drama. On the other hand, specialists in poetry and
prose have often been dismissive of medieval plays.[8] The isolation of the
drama as a special case was given authoritative approval by the Oxford
History of English Literature: C. S. Lewis's *The Sixteenth Century (excluding
the Drama)* set the seal on the dislocation already achieved by the publication of the history of fifteenth-century literature in two separate volumes.[9]
One reason for this latter oddity was the pious one of allowing E. K.
Chambers to write a miscellany, but the other was 'that the story of the
medieval drama and the story of the ballad are better told without strict
attention to the boundaries of time'.[10] Well, of course, one cannot know
enough about medieval drama to be strict about time, it is true, but one
can try, and the lack of evidence is all the more reason why one should not
ignore the signs that medieval plays had a good deal in common with
other forms of literature being written in the fourteenth and fifteenth
centuries.

   The one form of literature which has been regularly connected with the
plays is the medieval sermon, though that is only since the pioneering
work of Owst, who scornfully wondered that the 'links between sermon
and drama . . . so long have escaped the notice of learned editor and
commentator, intent upon the task of tracing the beginnings of modern
dramatic art in this country.'[11] Owst brought evidence to show that not
only raw subject-matter but also free treatment of sacred episodes, with
dramatic intensity and humour, was common in contemporary sermons,
and backed up his view that:

. . . scholarship has been sadly led astray by lack of acquaintance with another and a much despised literature which had already set forth in true and satisfying combination the colloquial, the proverbial, the jovial and the religious.[12]

Modern scholars have followed Owst at least as far as seeing the connection, but many have simply considered the sermons as source-material for the plays. Particular interpretations of Scripture, uses of Apocryphal matter, themes and symbols have been studied, but little notice has been taken of the implications of Owst's words for the style, tone and range of feeling in the plays. One can at least see, if one approaches the plays in terms of their source-material in Scripture and in sermon-literature, rather than in terms of 'a form of art springing fundamentally from the lives of the people',[13] how the basic staple of medieval plays came to be a combination of narrative and declamation. To the sequence of speeches necessary for the unfolding of the Scriptural episode has been added the voice of the teacher, who both identifies and explains in a purely didactic role and also exhorts and warns in a homiletic one.

There are other literary connections which help one understand the nature of medieval plays. These are parallels rather than origins (though sources may be involved), sometimes in the area of subject-matter and ideas, sometimes in the area of form and style. The simple, obvious parallels are between the plays and contemporary lyric and narrative poetry on religious, moral and Scriptural themes. Passion lyrics, laments of the Blessed Virgin, mortality lyrics expressing the regrets of age, all provided instances of the interpretation of religious ideas through feeling, metrically and affectively expressed. Many of the lyrics, including secular ones on such topics as the abuses of the age, the wickedness of women and the follies of fashion, were expressed in direct speech, sometimes as if 'spoken' by the poet, sometimes as dramatic monologues, or actually as dialogue in such poems as the dialogue for Christ and Mary 'Stonde wel, moder, under rode'. Dialogue and monologue are a major feature also of the narrative poetry of the period, so that the relationship between drama and narrative poetry is not only a matter of the use of particular poems (such as the dependence of the Chester playwright on *The Stanzaic Life of Christ*)[14] but also a question of imitation of style. The *Gawain*-poet's versions of Old Testament narratives, especially in *Purity*, provide vivid realisations of Scriptural scenes through description, some fine dialogue (as in the scene between God and Abraham) and speeches of authority and power for God and of tyrannical rant for Nebuchadnezzar and Belshazzar from which northern playwrights could well have developed dramatic renderings of the Almighty, Lucifer and Herod.[15]

The connections between medieval plays and other forms of literature which do not share subject-matter with the drama are more tenuous, but there are many suggestive parallels which deserve fuller exploration than is appropriate here. One is the medieval interest in debate literature, where one finds both the idea of dramatic form and the interest in expressing opposing attitudes, including some of the moral antitheses which are the basis of plays. *The Debate between the Soul and Body* and the alliterative poem *Death and Life*, for instance, are expressions of the philosophy which sees life as a diametrical opposition between the values of earth and of heaven, while *Winner and Waster* and the poems of the 'parliament' tradition (*The Parliament of the Three Ages*, *The Parliament of Fowls*, the Prologue to *Piers Plowman*) explore the contrary values of men of different classes, different ages and different temperaments. Overlapping with the dramatic interest of debate-poems are the many allegorical narratives (mainly dream-poems) of the fourteenth and fifteenth centuries. By means of the description of emblems and abstractions and the invention of speeches for personifications, poets express the contraries within the human mind and within the society in which men pass their mortal lives. Nature and the sublunary world is the main setting and human nature the main subject. The tension between reason and feeling within the mind mirrors the opposition between sanctity and sin in man's behaviour and between selfless other-worldliness and greed for money and power in the world at large.

In the greatest of medieval English dream-poems Langland provides the bridge between moral allegory and Scriptural narrative, and his dreams are often in the form of vividly dramatised scenes, monologues and dialogues. The trial of Lady Meed, the confessions of the Deadly Sins, the Harrowing of Hell, the building and defence of the Barn of Unity are all cast in a semi-dramatic form; strong characterisation and dramatic tension are conveyed as well as a focusing of the ideas through speech. Langland has a claim to being the greatest medieval English dramatist and it is surprising that no-one has created a stage drama from *Piers Plowman*. Not only is his version of the Harrowing of Hell superior in power and bite to the versions in the cycles, but he is the one writer who can combine in personified abstractions the representative symbolism with vivid immediacy. Of Langland's fifteenth-century successor Lydgate the same cannot be said, but he was essentially a middlebrow populariser and he is important as the one who continued the line of allegorical writing about the life of man and passed on the tradition to later poets such as Skelton, who is another 'bridge' poet, since in his poem *The Bowge of Court* and his play *Magnificence* we see the extent of overlap between vision and drama.

Even in the secular epic and romance literature of the Middle English period there are interesting connections with the plays. Both Scriptural and allegorical dramas often present the figures of kings, knights, courtiers, messengers and servants which make up the cast-list of medieval chivalrous romances, and make use of some of the stock situations and scenes of secular narrative – banquets or public assemblies, for instance, in which a king receives messenger or challenge and issues commands to courtiers and servants. From the tradition of Christ as a chivalrous knight who defends his lady (the soul) in tournament (the Crucifixion), the drama can draw imagery and association. The romance themes of threatened innocence, the humbling of pride, trial by ordeal, the quest and journey as a moral test, and so on can be attached to Scriptural figures whose situation makes them appropriate, and they can also be used to give particularity and association to the allegorical representative of man in the moral plays. So Mary can appear in the role of the slandered virtuous maiden and Mankind can show his worldly ambition through the accessories of knighthood. Many of the late romances, in any case, show adventure turned into moral episode; in the late fourteenth-century alliterative poem *The Awntyrs of Arthur*, for example, Guenevere, out hunting with Gawain, meets the ghost of her mother, blackened by fire and covered with toads and snakes, who has come to warn her daughter of the punishments awaiting her if she continues a life of sin.[16] Courtly narratives are also, like moral plays, often instructive instances of the vagaries of Fortune. Fifteenth-century interest in educational literature shows itself as much in moralisation of romance tales as in the dramatisation of moral episodes and the combination of Scriptural narrative and homily.

The moral plays, on which this study will concentrate, are thus neither, in my view, a completely distinct kind of drama, nor even a completely distinct type of literature. There are many overlaps with sermons, lyric and narrative poems and so on, which show common subject-matter, common rhetorical uses of speech and dialogue and common themes – themes which can emerge from very different kinds of illustration. One has also to reckon that the plays overlap with some non-literary traditions, where the evidence is very scattered and fragmentary, such as forms of court entertainment – tournaments, courtly games, disguises and ceremonies. The writers of plays drew on these traditions, sometimes as ways of spicing instructive drama with familiar amusement, but we can only know the traditions from the uses to which the drama put them, whereas with literary traditions, one has the written evidence of non-dramatic work. The chapters that follow will concentrate on plays, but, since I want to try to show that the plays are more varied than they have been thought, and that they can appropriately be regarded as examples of the basic dramatic kinds, not as circumscribed by special medieval categories labelled 'morality play', 'mystery play' and so on, I will indicate the areas of non-dramatic writing which seem to me to provide a background to the themes and techniques of each of the four plays in turn.

CHAPTER TWO

Pride, Death and Tragedy

1. *The Pride of Life*

The Pride of Life is the usual title for some fragments of a fourteenth-century play, which once existed in an Irish manuscript. The manuscript was lost during the political troubles of 1922, when the Public Records Office in Dublin was destroyed by explosion and fire. We know the text only as it was published in 1891, a prologue and two episodes which amount to 502 lines of a play which must originally have been about twice that length.[1] As with the fragmentary text of the Old English elegy for the lost past, *The Ruin*, so with *The Pride of Life*; to a literary work about time and mortality history has added its own irony.

The play seems more complete than it is because the Prologue gives a lengthy summary (112 lines in 4-line rhyming stanzas) of the content of the whole. After the opening call for attention, the Prologue promises that we shall hear of the King of Life:

> In pride and likinge his life he ledith,
> Lordlich he lokith with eye;
> Prince and dukis, he seith, him dredith,
> He dredith no deth for to deye.
>
> (25–8)

His queen, who 'is lettrit in lor', bids him beware, but her advice, we are told, is rejected, as is that of the bishop. The King then sends a challenge to Death. (This is as far as the subsequent play gets.) The summary then indicates that Death comes and conquers Life:

> He dredith nothing his knightis;
> And delith him depe dethis wounde
> And kith on him his mightis.
>
> (90–2)

After death the soul, taken by fiends, has to be rescued by the intercession of Mary; the prologue ends with a prayer to the audience to be courteous and 'distourbith noght oure place'.

In the first of the two episodes of the play proper, the dramatist first presents his central figure, *Rex Vivus*, the King of Life, boasting of his power:

15

> King ic am, kinde of kingis ikorre,
> Al the worlde wide to welde at my wil.
> (121–2)

Then the Queen professes loyalty (with a touch of Mrs Micawber) and the King's bodyguard, the two knights Strength and Health, express theirs. This is the status quo of the play:

> Qwherof schuld I drede
> Qwhen I am King of Life?
> (171–2)

To the puppet-like opening the Queen's reminder to the King to prepare his soul for death brings the sting of dramatic life; the dialogue quickens into bitter opposition:

> *Rex*   Woldistou that I were dede
> That thou might have a new? . . .   (195–6)
> I ne schal never deye
> For I am King of Life . . .   (211–2)

> *Regina* I rede ye serve God Almighte
> Bothe loude and stille.
> This world is bot fantasye
> And ful of trechurye.   (229–32)

The King's *amour-propre* is bolstered by Strength, Health and his messenger, who is called both Mirth and Solas, who flatters and reassures:

> I have ben bothe fer and nere
> In bataile and in strife;
> Ocke ther was never thy pere,
> For thou art King of Life.   (291–4)

In the second episode the Queen sends for the Bishop and (after a gap in the text) the Bishop has a lengthy homiletic speech expressing the common medieval theme of the mutability of the world, by means of reversals of virtue into vice. This tradition, based upon the medieval Latin topic of 'The Twelve Abuses of the Age', is familiar in complaint and turns up in several medieval plays, often with satirical intent.[2] Here the Bishop's condemnation of a corrupt and heedless age provides another static opening which is then galvanised into life by the vehemence of the two opposing views of Bishop and King:

> *Episcopus* Schir Kyng, thing oppon thin end
> And hou that thou schalt dey! . . .   (391–2)

> *Rex*   Wat! bissop, Byssop Babler!
> Schold Y of Det have dred? . . .   (407–8)

Episcopus	Qwhen thou art graven on grene,
	Ther metis fleys and molde,
	Then helpith litil, I wene,
	Thi gay crown of golde.
	Sire Kyng, have goday,
	Crist I you beteche.
Rex	Fare wel, bisschop, thi way,
	And lerne bet to preche. (443–50)

This tart exchange leads to the King's despatch of his messenger to challenge Death, and with the messenger's boasting and threatening speech, the fragment ends.

As a play *The Pride of Life* is suggestive rather than accomplished. Because it is early and, even more, because it is unfinished, it seems embryonic. It is more interesting than its literal content might seem to warrant, because of its connections, possible origins and future developments; as some of Scarlatti's more experimental sonatas are enriched by the hearer's sense that implicit within them are the harmonies of later composers, so, on a more modest scale, with *The Pride of Life*. Rex Vivus is the model for many subsequent proud tyrants and scornful hedonists; in him is both the human lack of foresight of the coming of death, which is the theme of *Everyman*, and, though he is a king only figuratively, that royal arrogance in worldly and bodily power which is asking to be brought down, which is a major theme in Elizabethan histories and tragedies. The proud, noble hero, the promised battle between life and death, the sense of bitter conflict and inevitability and the archetypal nature of the figures are all the material of medieval tragedy.

Not all is potential, however. Though the play is short, it is dense and achieves a number of positive effects. The allegory is economical and allusive. The characterisation of Health and Strength as knights draws on the stock associations of chivalry, and colours the reader's expectation of the contest between life and death with the atmosphere of medieval warfare and courtly tournament. In the figure of the Queen the combination of loving submission to her husband and an independent moral guardianship, coming from book-learning and closeness to the church, sketches the outline of a court history which we can fill in for ourselves. The King's own folly, similarly, links with his love of 'mirth and of solas' and his ready abuse of others to suggest many a story already present in our minds. It is the world of medieval secular narrative verse, the romances of court life, that the author draws on and envisages as the actual setting of his allegory. The characterisation and expression bring similar associations to mind. The most effective dramatic quality in the work is the vigour of the dialogue, and this comes mainly from the characterisation of the king himself as abusively scornful of opposition. This portrayal resembles that of many tyrannical figures in romance. The forthright speech of Rex Vivus could well have sprung from the style of direct speech in such popular romances as *Havelok the Dane*, and from such characters as the bad-tempered Earl who is at odds with his wife, daughter and future son-in-law for much of *Sir Degrevant*, and whose family feelings are mainly expressed in terse, angry dialogue. The idiom, too, is close to secular narrative styles, and the folk-tale quality of the play comes partly from the simple verse-form, which has the rhythm and rhyme pattern of ballad metre for much of the play. It uses many of the features of the style of ballad and popular romance. So, for instance, one finds recurrent phrases (with something of the effect of refrain, as may be seen in the quotations above with variations on the line 'For I am King of Life'), and stock phrases such as 'both young and old', 'in breadth and in length', and many alliterative phrases, such as 'within sea and sands' and 'Thou art lord of limb and life'.

The themes of the play are also redolent of non-dramatic poetry. There is, in fact, no strong sense of the stage about *The Pride of Life*. Dialogue and monologue are used, but not so very differently from their use in narrative or dream poetry that one could not think of the play as a debate-poem. Another embryonic quality is just this suggestion of a bridge crossing from poetry to drama. The themes suggest a background partly of lyric poetry, in the reminders of poems of the *Ubi Sunt* tradition in the speeches of the Queen and Bishop about the transience of life. The use of the opposition between two allegorical figures is close to alliterative debate-poems. The early fifteenth-century poem called *Death and Life* (which survives only in a corrupt post-medieval copy) is closest in theme, but it is the general idea of the poem rather than any specific detail which suggests the sharing of a background with *The Pride of Life*.[3] Lady Life and Lady Death present their cases against one another and in their own defence and provide opposite poles between which the life of man and the understanding of mortality may be examined. Allegory, romance and Scripture come together in Death's proof of her power. First comes the general truth:

> Never any man upon mold any mirth had,
> That leeped away with thee, Liffe, and laughed me to scorne,
> But I dang them with my dints unto the deaffe earthe.
>
> (323–5)

Then comes the list of those brought down by Death, starting with Adam and moving on through the Old Testament to Alexander and other famous heroes:

> Arthur of England, and Hector the keene,
> Both Lancelott and Leonadas with other leeds manye,
> And Gallahault the good knight, and Gawaine the hynde,
> And all the rowte I rent from the Round Table.
>
> (338–41)

Finally, and most imaginatively, Death claims her power over the Son of God:

> 'Have not I justed gentlye with Jesu of heaven?
> He was frayd of my face in freshest of time,
> Yett I knocked him on the crosse and carved through his hart.'
> And with that shee cast of her crowne, and kneeled downe lowe,
> When she nemned the name of that noble prince.
>
> (345–9)

This claim is, in the debate, her undoing since Life then challenges her with Christ's Harrowing of Hell, seen as a defeat of Death:

> Death, thou daredst (*trembled*) that day and durst not be seene.   (418)

Unexpectedly, it is Death who is accused of bombast:

> And now thou prickes for pride, praising thy selven.   (429)

The poet has resolved this debate by allowing Life to extend her realm beyond the temporal world and become 'Everlasting Life' and to equate Death with Hell and the Devil.

This is a solution which is possible in *The Pride of Life*, but according to the prologue the conclusion would have followed the course apparent in the later dramatic treatments of the coming of death in *The Castle of Perseverance* and *Everyman*, which is to equate life with the body and to end the play with the question of the damnation or salvation of the soul. In this aspect of *Death and Life* lies the whole problem of medieval tragedy; I will return to it later.

The common concerns of drama and allegorical dream poetry are apparent also in the personifications of the Ages of Man in *The Parliament of the Three Ages*, from which one can see the closeness to traditions of Youth of the boastful zest of health and strength of the King of Life;[4] even the less immediately relevant *Winner and Waster* provides images of temporal pride challenged by principles of thrift, and a sense of the limitations of vain earthly pleasures, which show the same basic ideas as in the play. Even more suggestive is Langland's characterisation of Life in Passus XX of the B-text of *Piers Plowman*:

> And thanne lough Lyf, and leet daggen hise clothes,
> And armed hym in haste in harlotes wordes,
> And heeld Holynesse a jape and Hendenesse a wastour,
> And leet Leautee a cherl and Lyere a fre man;
> Conscience and counseil, he counted it folye.
>   Thus relyede Lif for a litel fortune,
> And prikked forth with Pride – preiseth he no vertue,
> Ne careth noght how Kynde slow, and shal come at the laste

And kille alle erthely creature save Conscience oone.
Lyf lepte aside and laughte hym a lemman.
'Heele and I,' quod he, 'and heighnesse of herte
Shal do thee noght drede neither deeth ne elde,
And to foryyte sorwe and yyve noght of synne.'

(Piers Plowman XX, 143–55)

Langland, like the preachers upon whose ideas he draws, emphasises the heedlessness of life, the blind folly which scorns thoughts of the spirit and the hereafter. This is one half of the personality of Rex Vivus and this is the half which belongs with the homiletic tradition of death plays of which *Everyman* is the best example. The other half is his metaphorical royalty which is characterised by boastful pride. The hero of *The Pride of Life* is to be disconcerted on both sides: to have his confidence in health and strength undermined and to be pushed off his regal eminence. The playwright has invested the basic diagram of Man versus Mortality with associations from lyric, narrative, allegory and debate to create a work, which, even in the fragmentary state in which it survives, has a suggestive richness. In some ways, the play has the quality of a folk-story about the doomed history of a mighty fool. Robert Potter points to the similarity between the King of Life and the bragging champion of folk drama and suggests the Mummers' plays have influenced it.[5] There are also interesting suggestions of a dramatised version of the game of chess, which occurs in several medieval works as an image of Fortune's chances.[6] King, Queen, Bishop and Knights form the main cast, the messenger with two names functions as outriding rooks, and the expected meeting between the white King of Life and the black King of Death would make the climax. The range of speculation is wide because of the lack of ending, which would have circumscribed the play, no doubt into a familiar didactic mould. The hero may be seen, as I have said, both as a King figure, whose pride is a preparation for a fall, and an Everyman figure, whose unheeding enjoyment of life is to be rudely interrupted by death. The former is the typical protagonist in medieval tragedy, and tragedy is the theme I wish to explore before turning to the latter.

2. *Tragedy*

The most familiar English expression of the medieval idea of tragedy is Chaucer's gloss in his translation of Boethius:

> Tragedy is to seyn a dite of a prosperite for a tyme that endith in wrecchidnesse.[7]

The idea is associated in Boethius with the variability of Fortune, who claims the right to give with one hand and take away with the other, since it is her nature to do so, and who reproves man for blaming his loss of worldly riches upon her:

> But the covetise of men, that mai not be stawnched – schal it bynde me to ben stedfast, syn that stidfastnesse is uncouth to my maneris? . . . I torne the whirlynge wheel with the turnynge sercle; I am glad to chaungen the loweste to the heyeste, and the heyeste to the loweste . . . What other thyng bywaylen the cryinges of tragedyes but oonly the dedes of Fortune, that with unwar strook overturneth the realmes of greet nobleye?[8]

In Boethius one finds both the idea of loss of happiness and of loss of position. It is the latter which is most emphasised in medieval writing. Boccaccio's *De Casibus Illustrium Virorum*, though it included other things, was taken as a model for narratives of major figures brought low by Fortune. Chaucer tries his hand at the series of 'De Casibus' tragedies in *The Monk's Tale* and displays the dull moral diagram which is produced by insisting that narratives all exemplify the same philosophical theme: men achieve great position; men lose great position; Fortune is fickle – Q.E.D. Chaucer's more interesting exploration of the Boethian idea of tragedy is in *Troilus and Criseyde*, where the loss of personal happiness rather than of power and wealth is at issue. Here the wheel of Fortune is an image turning through the poem, but Chaucer does not limit his tragedy merely to illustration of the pattern of mutability. Through the expansive treatment of the story (very different from the summaries in *The Monk's Tale*) Chaucer introduces complexities. He devotes much time to lyrical monologues about feeling and to invention of scenes in direct speech in which the uncertainties of the moment-by-moment unfolding of the story may be acted out. The result is that the working out of the tragic pattern, inevitable and seen from the start, is more moving than instructive. At the end the reader accepts that earthly love and all things of earth are unstable but looks back with regret at the fair of the world 'which passeth soone as floures faire'.

The other great English narrative tragedy of the medieval period, Malory's *Morte D'Arthur*, does concern itself with Fortune's overturning of 'the realmes of greet nobleye', but the work's power to move the reader depends little on its illustration of the fickleness of worldly fame, though that theme is present. Malory, like Chaucer, expressed the positive values of worldly life, here in the ideals of chivalry and love, and stable, noble government, with sufficient sympathy for the reader to be drawn into uncertainty when loyalties come into conflict, and to experience the tension between feeling and reason upon which a sense of tragedy depends.

Chaucer showed through the comments of the Knight and the Host on *The Monk's Tale* his sensible awareness of the depressing nature of continual exemplification of Fortune's malice:

> I seye for me, it is a greet disese,
> Whereas men han been in greet welthe and ese,
> To heeren of hire sodeyn fal, allas![9]

Fifteenth-century writers also showed, in various ways, a sense that tragedy was not merely a sequence of wealth and poverty which showed all men to be puppets in the hands of chance. Malory developed his, perhaps by blessed accident, by working within the framework of a traditional story of the rise and fall of a king and a society of the past, and by concentrating on making the story dramatic and clear and not worrying too much about improving moral messages. Lydgate took the other course and in *The Fall of Princes* presented a version of the fall of great ones which placed greater emphasis on cause and effect; rather than the mutability of life, he illustrates the mutability of men, retribution and poetic justice:

> And to pryncis, for thei be nat stable,
> Fortune ful oft, for al ther gret estat,
> Unwarli chaungeth and seith to hem chekmat.
>
> (180–2)

The point of view varies in the treatment of the actual narratives, since it fits wicked men rather more readily than virtuous, but Lydgate can find a moral in most things, of one sort or another.

> Pryncis, considrith in marciall policye
> Is nouther trust, faith nor affiaunce;
> All stant in chaunge, wt twynkeling of an eye.
> Up towarde heven sett your attendaunce!
> The worlde unsure and all worldlye plesaunce,
> Lordshipp abitt nat. Recorde on Julyus,
> Moordrid at Rome bi Brutus Cassyus!
>
> (2913–19)

It is sins against the Christian religion (heresy, the sins of Julian the Apostate and Mohammed) for which Lydgate reserves his strongest punishments and moralisations and, in this connection, W. Farnham sums up Lydgate's treatment of tragedy as follows:

> Lydgate is almost always incapable of a view of tragedy which gives suffering some traceable cause in human character without making the cause a simple sin easily classified.[10]

Farnham speaks elsewhere of Lydgate's limitations and sees him, in comparison with Boccaccio and Chaucer, as 'far less perceptive of life's complexity'. There is no more complexity in his other contribution to medieval tragedy, or rather to Death literature, his translation from

French of the *Danse Macabre*.[11] This too is schematic and patterned, a series of pairs of stanzas in direct speech, in which Death addresses his victims one by one, from Pope to child, clerk and hermit, and the victim responds. Here is Death to the King:

> O noble kyng, moste worthie of renoun,
> Come forthe anone, for al youre worthinesse . . .
> Who moste aboundith here in greet ricches
> Shal bere with him but a single shete.
>
> (105–12)

The King's reply is the inevitable immediate acceptance of Death's power:

> . . . I see, by clere demonstraunce,
> What pride is worth, force or hy lynage:
> Death al fordothe; this is his usage.
>
> (115–7)

It is Lydgate's idea of the tragic fall that one meets most often in the drama of the fifteenth century. There is a sense that to be worthy of literary expression the loss of happiness needs to illustrate a moral even if only that pride precedes a fall, and that worldly joy is built on sand. In using kings and other great men as central figures medieval tragedies overlap with those of other periods in the idea that greatness of position, vast wealth and power, greatness of ambition, and even greatness of soul enlarge the stories of loss and death into something stirring, universally significant and awesome. But in most dramatic examples worldly great-ness is viewed unsympathetically and only in terms of pride which can be brought down. Thus in both the cycles and the moral plays (and others) pride and fall make a standard moral pattern which may be used to characterise any non-virtuous noble, or man in position of temporal power. This would make a dreary uniformity of characterisation, were it not that medieval dramatists were particularly good at boasting speeches, and obviously enjoyed expressing self-praise and scornful rage, some-times as a linguistic tour-de-force. Lucifer, Herod and Pilate were the three main figures characterised in this way, but other demons, the world and the flesh, the Emperor Tiberius and various other figures in the Digby play of *Mary Magdalene*, and even Paul in the early stages of *The Conversion of St Paul* are given speeches expressing pride in their beauty, power, possessions, cleverness, and all the other aspects of 'the pride of life'.[12]

It is in the plays about Herod that one can best see the interpretation of Scriptural material as a moral pattern of tragic retribution, since in several of the plays the dramatists not only use their inventive energies on some splendid raging and ranting, but also return, after the Massacre of the Innocents, to give an account of Herod's death as punishment for his crime. In the Digby play *The Killing of the Children* Herod proclaims himself from the start as Fortune's favourite:

> Above all Kynges under the clowdys cristall
> Royally I reigne in welthe without woo;
> Of pleasaunt prosperyte I lakke non at all;
> Fortune, I fynde, that she is not my foo.
>
> (57–60)

When Watkyn, a comic soldier, gives him the news of the massacre and tells him that the mothers are cursing him in the streets, total reversal occurs:

> Oute, I am madde; my wyttes be ner goon,
> I am wo for the workyng of this werke wylde,
> For as wele I have slayn my frendes as my foon;
> Wherefore I fere, deth hath me begyled.
>
> (365–8)

He quakes, cries out to Mahomet and dies on stage. Here is the classic pattern of favour and loss, and of height and depth, with the two supernatural powers who are both allies and opponents, Fortune with her fickle favours and Death, the conqueror and betrayer.

Chester's Herod, who greets the Magi in true courtly style in French, is also invested with the characteristics of personified Pride:

> I Kinge of Kinges, non soe keene;
> I soveraigne syre, as well is seene;
> I tyrant that maye both take and teene
> Castell, towre and towne!
> I weld this world withouten weene;
> I beate all those unbuxome binne;
> I drive the devills all bydeene
> Deepe in hell adowne.
> For I am Kinge of all mankynde;
> I byd, I beate, I loose, I bynde;
> I maister the moone. Take this in mind –
> That I am most of myght.
>
> (Chester Play VIII, 169–80)

With some neat flourishes of insult and threat, the playwright portrays his fury at hearing the Old Testament prophecies of the Saviour, his malice against the three kings, his raging thirst, and the ordering of the massacre, before bringing retribution home in the form of the body of his own son. A rare touch of feeling brings the moment to life, as Herod protests to the child's foster-mother:

> He was right sycker in silke araye,
> In gould and pyrrie that was so gaye.
> They might well knowe by this daye
> He was a kinges sonne.

> What the divell is this to saye?
> Whye weare thy wyttes soe farre awaye?
> Could thow not speake? Could thou not praye
> And say yt was my sonne?   (Chester Play X, 409–16)

Again the punishment is immediate: Herod feels himself attacked by disease and sees swarms of fiends; he dies and a demon appears to take him to hell.

The most famous of the medieval Herod plays, *The Death of Herod* in the N-Town cycle, is thus based on a familiar enough idea, but the treatment of the idea is bold and imaginative. In the preceding pageant Herod's claims of power extend beyond earth even to heaven:

> I dynge with my dowtynes the devyl down to helle,
> For bothe of hevyn and of herth I am kyng sertayn.
> (N-Town cycle, Play 18, 7–8)

He is particularly vain of his beauty and fine kingly raiment, and when the massacre has been effected is full of glee and promises:

> Ye xul have stedys
> To your medys,
> Londys and ledys,
> Fryth and fe.   (N-Town cycle, Play 20, 121–4)

The playwright takes more trouble to establish the extent of Herod's decadence and callousness, and shows him glorying in his triumph by ordering an extravagant banquet:

> Beste metys and wurthyest wynes loke that ye non spare,
> Thow that a lytyl pynt xulde coste a thowsand pownde.
> Brynge alweye of the beste, for coste take ye no care.
> Anon that it be done!   (Play 20, 147–50)

And so the playwright prepares for his coup-de-theatre by setting up a feast of hysterical mirth, as the *Gawain*-poet does in his realisation of Belshazzar's Feast in *Purity*. At the very height of mirth, when, as the poet said in the Vernon lyric,[13] 'men beoth muriest at heor mele', Death enters, unseen by Herod, and speaks as God's messenger, scorning Herod's claims to power and instead proclaiming his own:

> I am sent fro God, Deth is my name.
> All thynge that is on ground I welde at my wylle . . .
> Ow se how prowdeley yon kaytyff sytt at mete;
> Of deth hath he no dowte; he wenyth to leve evyr-more.
> To hym wyl I go . . .
> (Play 20, 181–96)

25

The Devil appears to carry Herod and his soldiers off and Death ends the play, speaking to the audience. The moral example is first made plain:

> Of King Herowde all men beware,
> That hath rejoycyd in pompe and pryde.   (246–7)

Then the warning becomes more universal:

> For be a man nevyr so sownde,
> Of helth in herte nevyr so wel,
> I come sodeynly within a stownde . . .
> Of my comyng no man is ware,
> For when men make most mery fare,
> Then sodeynly I cast hem in care.   (263–70)

The play ends with a third powerful stanza, reminding us that we shall all be reduced to Death's state, worm-eaten and bare:

> Amongys wormys as I yow telle,
> Under the erth xul ye dwelle,
> And thei xul etyn both flesch and felle
> As thei have don me.   (281–4)

This fine ending takes *The Death of Herod* beyond the other Herod plays, since we are made to see not only evil pride brought low, but also our human kinship with Herod. This is the play that *The Pride of Life* might have been. The overlapping between Scriptural drama and 'morality play' is absolute here: history flows naturally into allegory and universality. Here too the play is not confined to the 'De Casibus' tragedy: pride and fall are the foundation of the play, but the dramatist's grafting onto the pageant the themes of mortality lyrics has brought us back to the combination found in *The Pride of Life* of the fall of a king and the universality of death.

The pattern of 'tragedy' visible in the Herod plays is an imitation of the pattern already demonstrated earlier in the cycles in the fall of Lucifer and the fall of Man, and the cases of Lucifer and Adam obviously fitted, better than that of Herod, the idea of 'a dite of a prosperite for a tyme'. However, the medieval dramatists were more concerned to display the reversal from prosperity to degradation than to explore the possibilities of the theme of loss of what was once noble in any extended or questioning way. Lucifer is displayed first in presumptuous boasts of his own beauty and power. His presumption in seeing himself as the source of light (Towneley version) and as God's equal is symbolically represented by his putting himself in God's seat. Immediately he falls (particularly swiftly and effectively in the York play) and all turns to the grotesque ugliness of Hell and the laments of the degraded devil, no fallen archangel but a malicious beast. The Fall of Adam follows the course of events in Genesis and confirms the pattern established by Lucifer's contradiction of God. The dramatists are, on the whole, no more interested in inventing scenes which would establish the prosperity and joy of Eden, than earlier in showing Lucifer before pride seized him. The aftermath of disobedience is shown through recrimination and bitterness and soon moves on to forecasts of the Redemption and the murder of Abel.

It is therefore the rather simple moral diagram of the fall from prosperity, which came as punishment for pride and disobedience, that is the main idea of tragedy used in the cycle plays. Because the emphasis was on punishment of sin, the fall of great ones turns into a stereotype of villainy. Lucifer set the pattern used later for Herod, and the power of the stereotype is obvious in its application to other ruling figures, as, for instance, to Pontius Pilate. It was possible for the medieval playwright to treat Pilate in a complex and interesting way, since he is a somewhat equivocal figure. In the influential Apocryphal text, the Gospel of Nicodemus, Pilate is shown to be a thoughtful man of troubled conscience. But in the Towneley Cycle one sees a preference for the cruder, stronger and more immediately stage-worthy idea of an evil and malicious Pilate. He is characterised by boasts of power, some flourishes of doggerel Latin ('sum dominus dominorum'), threats and corruption of the law. The York dramatist attempts to combine this demonic stereotype with the tradition of Pilate as a well-meaning but weak man, but to explore the doubtful success of that venture would take me away from the idea of tragedy and the development by fifteenth-century dramatists of the themes of *The Pride of Life*.

If one seeks in the medieval plays an idea of tragedy which moves, as Chaucer did in *Troilus and Criseyde* and as Malory did, beyond the moral lesson that Fortune and Death bring inevitable punishment for pride, one finds gestures and pointers rather than arrivals. Clearly, in the working out of the consequences of the Fall of Man there is a sense of the tragedy of loss, and one is never in doubt of the high seriousness of the medieval dramatists, but the idea of loss is there to prepare for the fulfilment of the Redemption and the righteousness of Judgment. There is even greater loss and horror in the life and death of Christ and in the scenes which reach their climax in the Crucifixion there are many of the qualities of tragedy. There is the inevitable fulfilment of a destined course. There is the sense of watching helplessly as an innocent figure is plotted against, unjustly tried, scorned and tortured. There is the painful revelation of the ugliness in human nature in the scenes of torture: the contrast between the silent dignity of Christ and the grotesque cruelty or callous indifference to barbarity of the judges, soldiers and torturers is poignantly used by several of the playwrights. There is also a much greater expression of sorrow in these scenes than in any other fifteenth-century drama, especially in the lamentations of Mary. Most significant of all one has in the figure of Christ the very essence of the ancient idea of hero, part god, part man; the human Christ can and must suffer death, and in the hapless enduring of the death necessary for others is a potentially tragic theme. But that is to look at it from a modern point of view; from the point of view of the Christian writers of the Middle Ages the whole sense of the meaning of Christian history was anti-tragedy; the Resurrection is the true climax. Farnham expressed it well, years ago:

> The Crucifixion could at the most be made to arouse a tragic pity for perfect goodness suffering ironically at the hands of lost creatures whom it had come to save; it could not be made to arouse the tragic terror that comes with the view of the hero helping to seal his own doom through imperfections recognisably like our own.[14]

This is the problem I referred to earlier with reference to the poem *Death and Life*. Tragedy needs the sense of an ending and once 'Life' is thought of as existing beyond death then tragedy turns into something else, 'divine comedy' at best, improving moral lessons at worst. The obvious conclusion is that medieval drama may be within the realm of tragedy, in its larger and not just in the medieval 'De Casibus' sense, but only as long as the play remains in this world.[15]

The main concepts of a tragic play which are possible, given this, and which are to some extent explored by fifteenth and early sixteenth-century dramatists are twofold. First there is the tragedy of free will: that is a play in which the choices made by the central character lead to tragic consequence and to the sense of waste and error. This is the tragedy which develops from the kingly aspect of Rex Vivus in *The Pride of Life* and which goes further than merely illustrating the punishment of presumption. It is the kind of play which connects medieval and Elizabethan drama, through the idea of the king as central character and the treatment of the human mind as composed of potentially warring elements and as the microcosm of the realm and of human society. The only play in the early period that in any sense (only a partial one) represents the type is Skelton's *Magnificence*. The second potential type of tragic play is the tragedy of realisation, in which loss of happiness consists of a stripping away of illusions. Death is the main instrument by which the vanity of earthly life is exposed and *Everyman* is the play within the period which comes nearest to fulfilment of the idea. This is the type of tragedy which develops from the other half of Rex Vivus, the human being's heedlessness of his moral state, and his aptness to worldly folly rather than mortal forethought. This too is the type of play which comes nearest (or could, if a playwright wished) to the sense of tragedy as a combination of the theme of the transitory earthly life and the expression of sorrowful experience and personal loss which Chaucer experimented with in *Troilus and Criseyde*.

If we look first at the tragedy of free will, then it is clear that in *Magnificence* Skelton drew, like the author of *The Pride of Life* before him, on the themes of medieval dream-poems, and on their interest in the moral debate enacted within man, and in the extension of that inner moral conflict to the outer conditions of things in human society. He had, when he wrote the play, already shown in his moral allegory *The Bowge of Court* how the Seven Deadly Sins could be converted into instruments by which the viciousness and folly of the life of the Tudor court could be exposed. His dreamer Dread, on a nightmare voyage on the ship of state, goes through a traumatic initiation into a world of greed, envy and suspicion. In the play we meet that world again, satirically personified in the grotesque quartet of intriguers, Counterfeit Countenance, Courtly Abusion, Cloaked Collusion and Crafty Conveyance. The relationship of the vice figures to the main character is, however, completely different in the play, since, instead of a vulnerable and naive dreamer, Skelton presents the case of a changeable ruler. The world of the court is examined in the spirit of literature intended as a 'mirror for princes', and Magnificence, the king at the heart of the play, is as much Henry VIII as he is the King of Life. The tragic possibilities of the play reside entirely in this central figure. Skelton conceives the play as 'A goodly interlude and a merry' and the comic illustration of the petty intrigues of the court, the lively realisation of Folly and Fancy and the use of literary parody give to the work a veneer of a laboured comedy of manners, but the main figure is in a different mode; Magnificence is a sketch for a tragic hero, and a bridge between the medieval toy of Fortune and Tamburlaine and Lear.[16]

At first sight, the play and its hero seem to belong firmly to the tradition of the 'De Casibus' tragedy. The choral epilogue in which Magnificence joins the virtues to express the moral of the play is a set of formal lyrics; each character has two stanzas which share a refrain pointing the mutability of the world. Circumspection's version is:

> Sodenly thus Fortune can both smyle and frowne,
> Sodenly set up, and sodenly caste downe.   (2524–5)

Perseverance's variation is:

> Today a lorde, tomorowe ly in the duste:
> Thus in this worlde there is no erthly truste.   (2538–9)

The process which has led to these conventional saws has all the symptoms of the stereotype. Magnificence at the height of his folly boasts of his superiority to all the great heroes of the past and of his immunity to Fortune:

> Fortune to her lawys can not abandune me;
> But I shall of Fortune rule the reyne.
> I fere nothynge Fortunes perplexyte.
> All Honour to me must nedys stowpe and lene.   (1459–62)

When Fortune casts him down it is in the *Ubi Sunt* mode that Magnificence rhetorically and repetitively laments, first in a stanza of apostrophe: 'O feble Fortune, O doulfull Destyny!' etc., and then in a stanza of rhetorical questions:

> Where is now my Welth and my noble estate?
> Where is now my treasure, my landes and my rent?   (2055–6)

But though there is much in the play that at a glance seems old-fashioned and laboured, static and repetitive, look again and one finds that there are originality and an active mind there too.

Skelton's focus is worldly and the beginning of the play is devoted to establishing a theory of government which is sensible. Magnificence begins in sanity and the establishment of the rule of Measure as the controller of Liberty starts the play off with an intelligible argument, which gives a completely temporal aspect to the king's later corruption, delusion and folly. Skelton's concern is how to win the gifts of Fortune and how difficult it is to keep them and to use them well. Skilfully he shows how it is from within the idea of nobility that corruption begins. Fancy (pretending to be Largesse) persuades Magnificence that it is proper for a prince to distribute gifts; people are calling him a miser:

> Thus in the talkynge of one and of oder,
> As men dare speke it hugger-mugger:
> 'A lorde a negarde! it is a shame!'   (386–8)

After an extraordinary length of time devoted to the vices (full of satirical point, ingenuity and variation in style and metre, but unbalancing the play) the process of corruption continues in the best part of the play, the scenes labelled by Ramsay 'Stage III, Delusion' (line 1375 ff.). Here Skelton devises a subtler and more interesting acting out of the process of delusion and corruption than the other dramatists of the period. The boasting speech already mentioned is not the climax, but only a stage in the process, which is followed by two ingenious scenes which show Skelton to have unexpected theatrical gifts.

In the first (line 1515 ff.) Courtly Abusion lures Magnificence with some elegantly phrased flattery, in which Skelton uses aureate language for its proper purpose, to indicate falsity and pretension, and with an alluring courtly picture of:

> a fayre maystresse
> That quyckly is envyved with rudyes of the rose,
> Inpurtured with fetures after your purpose,
> The streynes of her veynes as asure inde blewe,
> Enbudded with beautye and colour fresshe of hewe.
> (1550–4)

In the second (line 1629 ff.) Skelton takes a leap forward in stagecraft by creating an ironic scene in which Cloaked Collusion tells lies to Magnificence while Measure waits watching at the door, out of earshot. The scene in which Othello in Measure's place watches Iago fooling him with Cassio is more complex and far more pointed, but Skelton's scene gives one an uncanny feeling of suddenly seeing within the dramatic situation a glimpse of the ironies that later tragedies develop. The scene is brought to a neat conclusion as Measure, deluded, approaches to win Magnificence's favour, and Magnificence, deluded too, shows his rejection of Measure both in what he says and, with the irony that personification allegory can produce, in acting without measure. His words indicate that moderation has left his mind and his rule:

> What, woldest thou, lurden, with me brawle agayne?
> Have hym hens, I say, out of my syght!   (1722–3)

So Skelton devises particularly interesting scenes to demonstrate the weakening of his protagonist; his skill is shown both in the creation of dramatic irony and in literary evocativeness. The downward path leading to folly, poverty and despair is, for once, plausible and expressed with some feeling and imagination. The degradation is handled well too: Magnificence is beaten down, despoiled of his goods and raiment, and preached over, not here by Death, but by the bringer-down within this world, Adversity:

> Thys losell was a lorde and lyvyd at his lust;
> And now lyke a lurden he lyeth in the duste.
> He knewe not hymselfe, his harte was so hye;
> Nowe is there no man that wyll set by hym a flye.
> He was wonte to boste, brage, and to brace;
> Nowe dare he not for shame loke one in the face.
> All worldly Welth for hym to lytell was;
> Nowe hath he ryght nought, naked as an asse.   (1886–93)

For a moment the 'dite of a prosperite for a tyme that endith in wrecchidnesse' has become a true tragedy of noble error and the spoiling of what once was fine. But the didactic process asserts itself and Skelton, despite the secularity of the earlier action, conscientiously takes Magnificence from Mischief, with knife and halter at the ready, to Good Hope, Redress, Sad Circumspection and Perseverance, and takes the play back into the pattern of warnings of the fickleness of Fortune.

Skelton was writing a warning for a fickle prince and it would hardly have been appropriate, even if it were a possibility, for Magnificence to have become a tragic hero. Death hovers only for a moment, and attention moves back to the moral for the worldly ruler. But Skelton has at least thought about life on this earth, instead of merely caricaturing and dismissing it, and has thought about the nature of kingship and made use of Aristotelian ideas about the nature of the good life, the quality of magnificence proper to a ruler, and the relationship between liberty and moderation. To develop the portrayal of royalty beyond the crude terms of boastful folly and to develop the drama of man's moral choices within the figure of a magnificent worldly prince is to take the drama towards the later tragedy and the later history play, as we see with hindsight. In terms of its own time, though it shows greater literary subtlety and experiment, it is a portent rather than a transforming masterpiece. *The Death of Herod* in the N-Town cycle is, despite the more limited treatment of human nature, and the more rigid didactic pattern of pride and punishment, a better play.

3. *Everyman*

Everyman is the most immediately impressive of the medieval moral plays, the one most often performed in modern times, and the one with which the whole idea of the moral play is synonymous. The word 'Everyman' has become an accepted term for all individual human beings, not only because we read the contents of his library, but because it expresses the sense of both the individual and the universal as none of the other personification-names does. The strength of *Everyman* as a play is that it deals with the common case. Its basis is the universal idea that is expressed in the most memorable line in medieval English drama:

> O Deth, thou comest whan I had thee leest in mynde!

The opening of the play is swift, strong and sure. God's condemnation of the sins of mankind ('In worldely ryches is all theyr mynde') leads quickly to the dispatch of the messenger Death, to summon Everyman to his reckoning, and to the start of Everyman's preparation for the journey he must make. The beginning establishes a pressure upon the central figure and an outcome to which the play must lead; there is therefore a strong sense of the fulfilling of an inevitable course about the play, and the sense of a gradually tightening trap which grips the audience's imagination. The process which follows is, if we see it in devotional terms, a prepara-tion for death, but in terms of the shared common experience which links the audience with the hero it is a stripping away of life's illusions. Everyman learns that friendship, family and possessions mean nothing in time of need. The allegorical journey for which Everyman seeks companions is seen neatly to represent the statement of accounts which he must make. The things which he has valued in the world prove not merely invisible assets but even debits on the balance-sheet of the soul. As he looks for something to put in the credit column, he finds his Good Deeds paralysed and bound; he is forced to examine his state and begins to come to realisation (personified in Knowledge). This leads to confession and penitence; that is, he learns to be honest about his own failings. His penance (self-scourging) releases Good Deeds from bondage to accompany him on his journey. As the relentless process to death is completed, he learns that his bodily favours and forces, Beauty, Strength, Discretion and Five Wits, will go from him, and that:

> All fleeth save Good Deedes.

Everyman prays for mercy, commends his soul to God and dies. Knowledge and an angel state that Everyman will be saved and the figure of the Doctour points the final moral to us:

> This morall men may have in mynde.
> Ye herers, take it of worth, olde and yonge,
> And forsake Pryde, for he deceyveth you in the ende;
> And remembre Beaute, V. Wyttes, Strength, and Dyscrecyon,
> They all at the last to Everyman forsake,
> Save his Good Dedes there dothe he take.   (902–7)

The play's concentration on the theme of the coming of death and preparation for it give it force and unity. The central image of a journey and the idea of the pain of leaving and saying good-bye to life add emotional appeal. The feeling of inevitability is a strong persuasion to the hearer to understand the play as tragedy. The painful acquisition of knowledge of self and the world is a tragic theme. The play has often been seen as stark, with an austere power. If we come to it from *The Pride of Life* and other medieval plays and poems about the coming of death, it seems, in some respects, the logical fulfilment of the concept of death as a challenge to life and the world; we can see in Death's summons the timeless idea of an arraignment before a court for crimes we did not know we had committed. It is the Kafkaesque element in the play that has the strongest grip, the sense that:

> the consciousness of approaching death, which plays a part in the repentance scenes of . . . the other moralities, is expanded into a controlling metaphor for the human situation.[17]

But of course the play answers its questions, and the terms in which it does so are those of medieval teaching about repentance. As the play's editor says:

> *Everyman* may be called a Lenten penitential play or an allegorical drama concerned with the Four Last Things (Death, Judgment, Heaven and Hell).

Within these limits it is a strongly dramatic presentation of the theme of death. But it would be quite wrong to give the play the status of a tragedy.[18]

The dramatic virtues of *Everyman* are those of tragedy. But they have been developed (by the author of the presumably original Dutch play) in the service of didacticism, and it is the didactic aim which is responsible also for the work's weaknesses. It has too many characters; they are necessary for the purposes of exposition but dramatically redundant. The relentless pressure of the beginning of the play loses its force in the middle as self-examination is diverted by the speeches of Confession, Knowledge and Five Wits. Giving the end to 'Doctour' shows a far less sure grasp on or interest in drama than the author of *The Death of Herod*, who had the sense to give Death the last word.

Neither *Everyman* nor *Magnificence* may then be fairly called 'tragedy' in the larger sense of the term. But it does not seem irrelevant to discuss them in the context of tragedy. They both, in different ways, grow from the tradition, visible over a hundred years earlier in *The Pride of Life*, of setting up an image of man's life in this world to be challenged, examined and judged. They show two different aspects of life, but both are part of the purpose of tragedy. In one is the idea of using a king as the central figure, with the effect of enlarging the consequence of the action, so that as the great ones of the earth are brought to the dust, the rest of the world sees itself in their shadow. The other way is to use a figure who represents all of us and who expresses the common experiences of life. In both cases it is the dramatist's purpose to examine and judge human conduct. In this purpose is another reminder of how the moral plays share aims and themes with medieval Scriptural drama. *Everyman* has often been seen as rather isolated from other medieval plays, except in the basic idea of the coming of death, and as different from most in its almost complete seriousness. But it shares ideas both with Scriptural plays about death and retribution and, more significantly, with the final plays in the cycles, the plays of the Last Judgment. In *Everyman* the writer is concerned with the individual reckoning, whereas the public reckoning is the culmination of the cycles, but the same ideas of rendering accounts and judging conduct are the central matter. David J. Leigh has pointed out the features that Doomsday plays share with moral plays.[19] Especially important is the use of allegorical, or universal figures to represent the human race; as in *Everyman*, the playwrights are dealing with everybody's future experience. In the Towneley version the playwright uses demons to remind us with satirical bite of the rich range of the sins of the damned, but the other versions treat the subject with power and solemnity. With the version in the Chester cycle we come back to the themes mentioned earlier in this chapter. At the beginning, as in *Everyman*, God condemns human sin before the dispatch of messengers (angels here) to summon man to the reckoning. In a Dance of Death sequence, Pope, Emperor, King, Queen and others appear to represent first the saved, and then the damned. In

the voice of Rex Damnatus we hear the King of Life, Herod and Everyman:

> When I was in my majestie,
> soveraigne of shyre and of cyttye,
> never did I good. In noe degree
> through me was any grace.
> Of poore had I never pittie.
> Sore ne sycke would I never see.
> Nowe have I languowre and they have lee.
> Alas, alas, alas!
>
> Wronge ever I wrought to eych wight.
> For pennyes, poore in payne I pight.
> Relygion I reaved agaynst the right.
> That (keenlye) nowe I knowe.
> Lecherye, I held hit light.
> In covetousenes my hart was clight.
> On(e) good deede in God his sight
> Nowe have I not to shewe.
>   (Chester Play XXIV, 245–60)

CHAPTER THREE

Mankind *and Medieval Comedy*

1. *Mankind*

Though *The Castle of Perseverance* is the earliest of the three plays in the Macro manuscript, it is *Mankind* which provides the best contrast to *Everyman*: whereas *Everyman* is almost entirely serious and consistently dignified, *Mankind* is often frivolous and subjects virtue to indignity and scorn. In the past it was often seen as a betrayal of the worth of morality drama. Chambers, for instance, saw it as 'an example of the morality in its decadence', 'a very degraded type of morality, aiming at entertainment rather than edification',[1] and these remarks echoed earlier ones, such as Smart's description of it as 'only a sham morality' and Pollard's dismissal of it as 'about as degraded a composition as can well be imagined' (a description which he later modified into 'the least seriously didactic of the Moralities').[2] The main reason for objections to the play was its scurrility, but critics also found the mockery of virtue distasteful and the virtuous character of Mercy ineffectual. The reputation of the play has improved in recent years. Sister M. P. Coogan stressed the play's penitential, Lenten character and its dependence on devotional tracts, especially *Jacob's Well*, for its homiletic material.[3] She justified the use of obscenity and mockery, claiming that by these means the playwright gave realism to the allegory, bringing it closer than other moral plays to 'the actual situations of life'.[4] The lesson of the play is delivered to Mankind in theory by Mercy, but it needs the experience of the comic scenes for the teaching to be given force. A number of other scholars have followed Coogan and argued that the play is serious, ambitious and intelligent; underlying the scurrilous surface is a clever treatment of the sin of Sloth, which uses the contrast between elevated, literary, Latinate expression and low-class obscenity, local references and colloquialism as the main way of bringing the conflict between virtue and vice home to its audience.[5]

Chambers and the earlier commentators were, however, right in seeing that such effectiveness as the play has is largely comic and satirical. It has been produced several times recently and proves entertaining and far more actable than the two better-known moral plays *Everyman* and *The Castle of Perseverance*.[6] The stumbling-block in modern performance is the role and language of Mercy. The most effective parts of the play are the scenes of slapstick and low-class comedy given to the vice-figures, New Guise, Nowadays and Nought and their leader Mischief, and the lively scene in which the demon Titivillus defeats the resolve of Mankind. As

Bernard Spivack put it, *Mankind* is an early example of 'dramatic verve on the part of evil'.[7] This is not to say that the play is decadent, though it is true that the playwright sinks to the level of the tavern brawl and the mindless guffaw, but to claim that the dramatist draws from the material of didactic tracts about sloth illustrative incidents, which shape the allegorical conflict into the pattern of stage comedy.

The play is undivided in the Macro manuscript. Eccles follows Furnivall's division into three scenes: I, 1–412 (at which point the stage is empty); II, 413–733 (at which point Mercy's re-entry after long absence creates a turning-point); and III, 734–914. The merit of this division is that it makes a clear diagram of the three phases of the play. The first phase begins and ends in virtue, moving from Mercy's long, homiletic, opening speech to the firm resolve of Mankind, as he resists temptation and puts the vices to flight. The second phase begins and ends with the Vices yelling and crying in exclamatory lamentation and riot, and its centre-piece is Titivillus' successful seduction of Mankind. The third phase begins and ends with the voice of Mercy, whose expressions of the weakness of man and the generosity of God enclose Mankind's despair and repentance. Robert Potter sees this as the classic pattern of the morality play:

> The life of humanity is seen to begin in a potential state of innocence but to lapse in the course of experience into an actual state of sin. This state of sin, in turn, is seen to lead by its own contradictions toward the possibility of a state of repentance.[8]

There is, in fact, no one pattern which accurately defines the nature of early moral plays; as Merle Fifield argues, they share themes and ideas, but develop their own structure.[9] However, Potter's description does fit *Mankind*, but is it the nature of a special genre called 'morality play' that he is defining? Is it not rather that he is defining the classic pattern of comedy? The encounter between innocence and experience, from which innocence emerges wiser, is basic to all social comedy, and in *Mankind* there is a strongly satirical cast which focuses homiletic intention on details of conduct and speech rather more specifically than in any of the other pre-1500 plays.

The foundation of the comic design is the antithesis between Mercy and the vicious characters. The opening scene of *Mankind* is unusual among medieval plays in spending so long establishing the two extremes of conduct before the entry of the central human figure who is the 'hero' of the play. The rest of the play is implicitly present in the opening scene, which establishes two contrary ways of speaking and two contrary ways of looking at the world. So, Mercy is dressed as a cleric, possibly a friar, and he speaks in an exaggeratedly lofty, literary tone. His opening speech is full of polysyllables, Latinisms and rhetorical gestures:

> O soverence, I beseche yow your condycyons to rectifye
> Ande wyth humylite and reverence to have a remocyon
> To this blyssyde prynce that owr nature doth glorifye,
> That ye may be partycypable of hys retribucyon.   (13–16)

This aureate language is difficult for us to judge. It now seems pompous and pretentious, but it is doubtful whether it did so in the fifteenth century. East Anglian writers in the latter half of the period showed a liking for resonant Lydgatean style, and it obviously stood for some as an ideal of 'posh' expression. In *Mankind* it is a strongly-characterised speech-style contrasted with the different social and moral register used by Mischief and the three Vices. They mock Mercy for his elevated speech and show us the alternative. Mercy's opening speech (in its content a characteristic homiletic opening, treating of sin, redemption and judgment) ends with the familiar metaphor of John the Baptist, 'The corn shall be saved, the chaff shall be brent'. Mischief's entry is immediately a challenge, both to Mercy's preaching in general and to this metaphor in particular:

> I beseche yow hertyly, leve your calcacyon.   (*threshing*)
> Leve yowr chaffe, leve yowr corn, leve yowr dalyacyon.
> Yowr wytt is lytyll, yowr hede ys mekyll,
> > ye are full of predycacyon.   (45–7)   (*preaching*)

In rejecting the Scriptural imagery of corn and chaff Mischief bases his judgment on practical experience (of a corn-thresher he has hired, who can speak authoritatively on corn and chaff and correct Mercy's inaccurate nonsense) and stands for literal meanings not metaphors. Mischief is interested in making sport and when, shortly after, he is reinforced by New Guise, Nowadays and Nought, the speeches become short, staccato ones full of jest, ribbing and challenge, accompanied by physical violence. They try to make Mercy take off his long clothes and dance, and then they trip him up and, in the midst of the knock-about, they identify themselves as representing the world, in the three-in-one idea of what their names represent: new fashion, up-to-the-minuteness and meaninglessness. Mercy characterises Nowadays' brusque greeting 'grett yow well' as 'few wordys, few and well sett!' (102), and this points to the difference between the amplitude of Mercy's style (which is also characteristic of much fifteenth-century poetry) and the down-to-earth, no-nonsense brevity of the Vices, which New Guise further describes:

> Ser, yt ys the new gyse and the new jett,
> Many wordys and schortely sett.
> > (103–4)

This presumably refers to such monosyllabic expression as is in line 103, ('ten dull words . . . in one dull line').

It is the audience's first impulse to prefer the laconic directness of the Vices' speech to Mercy's repetitions and inflations, as Paula Neuss has argued, but, as the play progresses, the short sharp speeches becomes more and more limited in their tedious literalness, jokey slang and, above all, their witless obscenity. The contrast develops soon from the offer of a new, curt style to sneering and mockery of Mercy's 'Englysch Laten' (124), which is put to the test by a joking challenge to Mercy to translate dirty talk. The descent of the tone of the dialogue into scurrility is almost immediately pointed out to the audience by Mercy's judgment:

> Thys ydyll language ye xall repent.
> (147)

The moral significance of words is amplified when Mercy later says:

> How may yt be excusyde befor the Justyce of all
> When for every ydyll worde we must yelde a reson?
> (172–3)

The reference to Matthew 12.36–7 ('by thy words thou shalt be condemned' etc.) adds Scriptural authority to the idea the dramatist has ingeniously established, that the style of speech is the outward expression of inner moral state.

The importance of establishing two antithetical languages at the beginning of the play is made clear when Mankind himself is shown to be capable of speaking both dialects. He begins with an elevated utterance akin to that of Mercy, but later loses the polysyllabic signs of sanctity and descends through a more neutral style into the idle gabble of the Vices:

> A tapster, a tapster! Stow, statt, stow!
> (729)

At the end he recovers his literary elevation in an ecstasy of aureation:

> A Mercy, my suavius solas and syngular recreatory,
> My predilecte spesyall, ye are worthy to hawe my lowe.
> (871–2)

The opening scene shows us, in stylistic terms, the range of possibilities for Mankind. Through the imagery of clothing also, which echoes the linguistic symbolism, the opening scene prefigures, in the jesting moment of the Vices' trying to take off Mercy's long robe, the later action of the play. Mankind's virtue is betokened by long, ample clothing as much as by long, ample words and the vices offer a curt, new style of dress when they cut the robe down into 'a fresch jakett after the new gyse' (676). The contrasts between spiritual and physical meanings, that is, between allegorical and literal, which are presented in the antithesis between

Mercy's words and those of his opponents are also ideas which are developed and built on in the rest of the play.

Once he has established the extreme of Mercy's style, the playwright modulates his language in the speech that precedes Mankind's entry (162–95). It is more direct and forceful, and it conveys a sense of deeper feeling, as when Mercy speaks of sinners having to render their account on Judgment Day:

> Then xall I, Mercy, begyn sore to wepe;
> Nother confort nor cownsell ther xall non be hade;
> But such as thei have sowyn, such xall thei repe.
> Thei be wanton now, but then xall thei be sade.
>
> (178–81)

The more forthright caring tone, with an echo of moral lyrics, establishes Mercy's role as father-confessor, ready to guide the uncertain Mankind. The latter's first speech (186–216) goes through the same modulation: he first uses Latinisms and polysyllabic rhyme-words, but after such flourishes in the opening eight lines, his language takes on the sober tone of moral analysis, such as is found in the more educated sermon of the period. Attention is directed to a new aspect of the conflict of opposites:

> My name is Mankynde. I have my composycyon
> Of a body and of a soull, of condycyon contrarye.
>
> (194–5)

The opposition of elements within Mankind is the internal equivalent of the antithesis already presented externally. Immediately one sees the connections between the opening scene and the sense of warring elements within human nature. As he contrasts the qualities of spirit and body, the dramatist infuses stronger feeling into Mankind's speech.

> O thou my sowl, so sotyll in thy substaunce,
> Alasse, what was thi fortune and thi chaunce
> To be assocyat wyth my flesch, that stynkying dunge-hyll?
> Lady, helpe!
>
> (202–5)

The effect of the scene between Mercy and Mankind which follows is well-imagined. The troubled doubt of Mankind gives to the familiar idea of the debate between the soul and the body enough of a sense of individual psychology for one to see him both as a representative of human nature and as a character, simple but serious, thoughtful and vulnerable. Mercy's speeches, though again setting forth some familiar medieval themes, pick up emotional resonance from echoes of contemporary lyrics about mortality and transience and about Christ as defender of the soul. The relationship between soul and body is expressed as a battle: to win it one must become a knight of Christ. Life is brief, – 'So helpe me Gode, yt ys but a chery tyme' – and moderation is the only way to live, or 'Mesure ys tresure', as Mercy puts it, echoing Lydgate and medieval lyrics and proverbs. The body is like a horse, which must not be over-fed lest it be ill-disciplined and unable to bear the soul to battle. This last image leads to sneering interruptions from the three Vices: they have not come on stage, and so, presumably, call out from the audience.[11] Their comments are literal-minded (they reject the metaphorical use of the example of the horse), abusive, quibbling and irrelevant. They repeat the effect of the first scene, in that Mercy is seen as tiresome, 'Because ye make no sporte' (268). Their jeers lead to the last part of the preparation of Mankind, Mercy's direct warning to be steadfast against temptation and to beware of New Guise, Nowadays and Nought, who will seek to corrupt him:

> Nyse in ther aray, in language thei be large;
> To perverte yowr condycyons all the menys xall be sowte.
>
> (295–6)

Their loose tongues represent one threat, but 'werst of them all' is Titivillus, who works invisibly by guile.

It is clear, from the careful preparation in these opening scenes for the trials of Mankind to follow, that *Mankind* is no example of drama in degeneracy, at least from the point of view of intelligent craftsmanship. The contrary states of good and evil have been imagined and given character and style. The expression of religious teaching is literary but, while exaggeratedly elevated and bookish in places, it can modulate into a sober forcefulness and, at times, into passionate and touching phrases of sorrow and anxiety. The playwright is clever enough to make apparent both the serious and the comic side of the learned preacher. On the other hand, the language of the Vices can have a forthright vigour, speed and racy tang, as well as crass vulgarity, barren literalness and meaningless gabble. The treatment of conduct is unusually intelligent and detailed. This marks the play as rooted in the realism of the medieval sermon and in the moral examination of social conditions and behaviour which is the essence of medieval satire. Though the moral rules are clear enough, the dramatist has created a sense of a free-for-all relationship between good and evil, through mockery, both on stage and from among the audience, and physical violence.

The antithetical structure of the play is most obvious and effective in the two temptation scenes at the centre of the play. In both, Mankind is attacked by the representatives of evil: in one he resists; in the other he succumbs. The relationship between the two scenes is self-evident in its broad effect; for the moral reversal necessary to the design of the play two opposite acts must be shown. But beyond that broad effect are a number of ingenious enrichments of the significance of the action, which give to the play its individual character.

First, there is interesting variation in the nature of the temptation offered in the two, and lively invention in the dramatisation of both. In the first scene (311–412) Mankind sets himself to eschew idleness by tilling the soil, and the temptation consists of the attempts of New Guise, Nowadays and Nought to distract him from honest toil. This they do with an obscene Christmas song, with interruption, mockery, scurrility, false sympathy and idle comment. The impression is of random teasing, continual niggling and needling which irritates Mankind into vigorous protest:

> Go and do your labor! Godd lett yow never the!
> Or wyth my spade I xall yow dynge, by the Holy Trynyte!
> Have ye non other man to moke, but ever me?
>
> (376–8)

The scene ends with his actual 'dinging' of the Vices, their howls and Mankind's thanks to God that he has been able to put his enemies to flight. This is probably the scene which has most dirty talk, which has seemed to some a gratuitous display of 'idle language'. It is a matter of opinion whether the device works or not, but one can see a consistent purpose in the dramatist's use of obscenity, particularly with reference to bodily functions. Just as the Vices' mockery of Mercy's erudition was expressed in their scornful challenge to him to translate 'turds' into Latin, so their attack on virtuous resolve is expressed largely in terms of the 'stinking dunghill' of the body. In New Guise, Nowadays and Nought the vanity of those who live in and for the world is presented as a sterility of the spirit, an inability to think in anything but physical and literal terms. This is the significance of one of their bodily jokes against Mankind when they suggest that he will make a good job of growing corn:

> Here xall be good corn, he may not mysse yt;
> If he wyll have reyn he may overpysse yt;
> And yf he wyll have compasse he may overblysse yt
> A lytyll wyth hys ars lyke.
>
> (372–5)

What they propose here is the ultimate in self-sufficiency, a cycle of life in which man's own urine and excrement provide the irrigation and compost necessary for the growth of food, to satisfy bodily hunger and keep the endless circle going. Here is a mocking version of the idea of physical existence as the be-all-and-end-all. The Vices are used as instruments of insult and derogation in the play, but they also represent the dramatist's satirical view of the world, and his sense of the nullity, and provincial narrowness of worldly values. Mankind's driving off of the vices represents a temporary defeat for the sordid triviality they embody.

In the second of the two temptation scenes (525–606) Mankind is attacked by a more formidable opponent, the demon Titivillus, skilled in lies and deceit, who is later identified simply as the Devil. This scene is more elaborately developed in stage terms than the earlier one, through props, physical action and the supposed invisibility of the demon. As Titivillus conceals a plank beneath the soil, confuses Mankind by hanging his net before his eyes, steals the corn, which Mankind has left on the ground, and watches in glee when Mankind's spade strikes the hidden board, and so on, there is plenty of lively fun to be enjoyed. The scene has also a stronger structural sequence than the rather random testing of Mankind by the forces of the World. Here Titivillus first tricks Mankind into giving up labour, by making the work of the body difficult and frustrating. Then he succeeds in making him give up prayer, again by exploiting the weakness of the body in convincing him that he must relieve his bodily needs in the yard. As Mankind succumbs to sleep, which represents the slothful contrary to the active spirit of prayer, Titivillus slanders Mercy, saying that he is a thief and a gallows-bird, and so brings about the third stage of Mankind's corruption: he believes ill of good, gives up hope and faith in Mercy, and sets off for the tavern and a life of debauchery. This scene (and the preceding scene with the Vices) is the only appearance of Titivillus, and it is a display of showmanship (enhanced, if, as has often been suggested, the part was played by the same actor as was playing Mercy, by a display of virtuosity). The character takes the audience into his confidence, offers them tips about passing false coins, and acts as commentator on his own plots and the significance of what he is doing. He sums up his achievement in his last line:

> For I have brought Mankynde to myscheff and to schame.
>
> (606)

The two temptation scenes are well contrasted also through the intelligent use of symbolism. Mankind's role in the play is identified as that of honest labourer by his spade, and the self-appointed task of avoiding idleness by digging and sowing. The dramatist does not need to explain the allegorical significance of any of this, since it is obvious enough, and connects with the earlier references in the play to corn and chaff, to sowing and reaping, to the fruits of labour, and so on. Mankind is, of course, the representative of Adam, who was furnished with a spade as a sign of his life of toil, after he was banished from Eden. Digging thus stands for the whole idea of man's penitential labours on this earth, as well as the idea of occupying oneself with useful tasks to fend off the Devil, and to earn salvation through virtuous acts, as one wins fruits from the earth by toil.

Spades turn up with symbolic meaning often in medieval pictures and instructional writings. For example, in the illustrations found in the presentation manuscript of the Latin play, *Liber Apologeticus*, which I will discuss in the next chapter, there is one picture of God handing to Man a scourge and a spade; in the text God explains that the spade is a sign of Man's loss of lordship over the earth, and will be a reminder, as Man tills the soil, that he is dust and unto dust he will return. (This is the text from the Book of Job which Mankind fastens to his breast, before he begins to dig – *Mankind* 315–22.) In the didactic text *Jacob's Well*, from which the dramatist probably drew some of the homiletic material for *Mankind*, the basic allegorical idea is that of digging out the accumulated slime and filth of sin from the well of grace, and the spade is given several different interpretations in the course of the work. In one chapter the spade is called 'cleanness', and the three parts of the spade are said to signify pure thought, clean speech and good works.[12] From such contemporary symbols and allegories it is evident that Mankind's spade carries moral significance. The activity of digging involves sufficiently distinct movements to make a good bit of mime or stage business, and it is effortlessly allegorical. When Mankind takes his spade as a weapon against the Vices, it is clear that labour is a defence against idle vice and that spades, like plough-shares, can be forged into swords against evil. The scene is physically lively, but its meaning is clearly figurative. In the scene with Titivillus, the dramatist ingeniously plays with one's sense of the relationship between physical action and figurative moral meaning. It is a clever exploitation of the idea that the body is the enemy of the soul that leads to his making the turning-point of the action the moment when Mankind's spade strikes the plank beneath the earth. Here resolution ends. And it is through the simple frustration of the literal, physical act of wielding the spade. So much for the figurative moral understanding of Mankind's digging, in the earlier scene. When it comes to the testing-point, it is the experience of the actual which proves the stumbling-block and the limitations of the flesh deflect the course of the spirit.

The central part of the play is, then, dominated by the forces of evil, which eventually overcome the virtuous intent which Mercy had planted in Mankind. The playwright gives a lot of attention to identifying the nature of vice in specific detail, especially by inventing comic business and using the possibilities of the theatre. After Mankind has driven off New Guise, Nowadays and Nought by hitting and injuring them with his spade, there is a comic scene in which Mischief acts as a parody of the consoling mother towards her three crying babes, and goes through a comic mime, which historians of drama have suggested was taken over from traditional Mummers' Plays, of supposedly chopping off Nowadays' head, and restoring it whole. More theatrical by-play precedes the entry of Titivillus, who is announced to the audience by his voice off, and by the Vices, who praise him to the audience and get them to give money if they want to enjoy 'hys abhomynabull presens'. The collection is another inheritance from the folk-play and is one of the items in the play which has suggested to some that this is 'popular' drama. But the use of the collection in connection with the Devil has the effect of parody: the Devil is made to seem like a side-show at a fair and the collection of money reduces his level to a commercial affair, which is re-inforced by the effect of anti-climax when Titivillus himself arrives with a flourish of Latin:

> Ego sum dominancium dominus and my name is Titivillus.
> (475)

and then immediately identifies the Vices to the audience as horsethieves and reveals that he himself is broke. This seems to me all quite sophisticated in intention. It is a clever way of *showing* the nature of evil rather than telling. The passage full of local references (502–24) in which Titivillus dispatches New Guise, Nowadays and Nought to prey on a roll-call of the inhabitants of East Anglia and Cambridgeshire, is similarly sophisticated, an 'in-joke' to be appreciated by an audience who would know all the names and find funny the idea of their contact with sin. Such devices show the dramatist's comic invention, and add to the realistic expression of the nature of sin and vice. Evil is close to home, is factually and literally identifiable; this is a way of showing what it means to be of the world. Instances of greed, theft and deceit, though presented in comic banter, gradually accumulate, and, after Mankind has yielded to temptation, they turn into an explicit catalogue of crimes. As the three Vices and Mischief enter through the audience (in itself a device to imply that the audience shares their nature), they bring jolly tales of their exploits, which we can in reality identify as horse-stealing, church-robbing, murder, prison-breaking, rape and theft. That Mankind should have been hypnotised by Titivillus into asking pardon of such as these is an irony crowned in the mock-court scene where Mischief compels Mankind to engage in an oath-swearing ceremony, in which he promises to be lecherous, to 'robbe, stell and kyll', to neglect to go to mass and to become a murdering bandit. In his new short jacket he becomes a ludicrous instance of the 'new guise', and the state of moral chaos into which he has descended is neatly enacted by the contrast between the unexpected sound of Mercy's voice off-stage, crying

> 'What how, Mankynde! Fle that felyschyppe, I yow prey!'
> (726)

and the riot on stage, which precedes Mercy's re-entry:

Myscheff   Hens away fro me, or I xall beschyte yow all.

New Gyse   What how, ostlere, hostlere! Lende ws a football!
         Whappe, whow! Anow, anow, anow, anow!

> (731–3)

There is fun in all this, obviously, but the fact that the audience welcomes the re-entry of Mercy, with the feeling of greeting an old, safe friend, is a recognition that the playwright knows what he is doing. He has always made clear the unsettling disorder that is identified with vice, as well as its barren and sordid vanity and criminality. The burlesque and mockery is enjoyable, as long as it is clear that it will be put in its place in the end.

The latter part of the play is nearest to the conventionally didactic, and here one finds passages and ideas which show closest resemblance to other plays and to Christian instruction-books on the nature of sin. A new phase of the action is marked by Mercy's long speech (734–71) of regret for Mankind's instability. This is a tissue of familiar ideas about mutability and frailty, expressed in Mercy's most ample and elevated style. However, if one can push one's way past the impression of fussiness, created by a rash of words such as *odybyll*, *dyspectuose* and by the pairing of synonyms ('thraldam and captyvyte', 'dyscomende and dysalow', etc.), one can see that, even here, the dramatist is not merely using the virtuous character as a homiletic mouthpiece. The speech is a lament, in which Mercy cries in sorrow for the weakness of men, and there are some sharp points in the midst of the verbal extravagance, particularly in the word-play on Mankind's name in:

> Man onkynde, wherever thou be! (742)

The vanity of the world, which has been fully demonstrated in the idleness of the Vices, is Mercy's theme:

> Vanitas vanitatum, all ys but a vanyte. (767)

This theme is intensified by the strong current of emotion running through the speech, which has its climax in Mercy's own stiffening resolve and the searching cry which ends the speech and sends him off-stage to seek Mankind:

> Xall I not fynde him? Yes, I hope. Now Gode by my proteccyon!
> My predylecte son, where be ye? Mankynde, *vbi es*? (770–71)

The conflict between virtue and vice is then briefly re-animated by Mischief's scornful imitation of Mercy's words:

> My prepotent fader, when ye sowpe, sowpe owt yowr messe,
> Ye ar all to-gloryede in yowr termys: ye make many a lesse.
> (772–3)

Again vice is associated with physical matters and with language appropriate to a child, in opposition to the overblown, glorified style of virtue. In the speeches that follow more comic Latin, doggerel rhyming and repetition, spiced with nitwittery and lavatorial humour, characterise the vicious characters and lead to the most evil act in the play, the attempt to persuade Mankind to suicide. The association between humour and evil is here at its blackest. The humour is of the slapstick kind as the vices attempt in a confused mêlée to get the rope round Mankind's neck and

New Guise nearly gets strangled while demonstrating how it should be done. The knockabout disorder is a curious counterpart to the disorder of spirit in Mankind, the depression that results from sin, the sloth of spirit which is the true centre of the medieval idea of *accidie*. This scene identifies the role of Mischief in the play as not only the sense of disorder and riot, but also the sense of grievous harm and even of suicide itself.[13] The scene is a brief re-enactment of what had happened earlier; the values of virtue and vice are again identified, partly by speech-styles and partly by the contrast between the feeling, caring speech of Mercy and the trivial callousness of the Vices' treatment of Mankind.

Once the Vices have been put to flight by Mercy's entry, the current of interest flows into the devotional stream of thought directed to the figure of Mankind, left lying on the ground in a state of despair. Mankind has to be encouraged to repentance and confession and to seek God's mercy. But the dramatist keeps up his attempt to render his material in stage terms by intensifying the impression of a crucial battle for the soul of Mankind through the latter's excessive contrition, which becomes obstinacy in sin, a belief that redemption and mercy are impossible. Mercy must therefore persuade him and overcome his stubborn despair. The homiletic material about the mercy of God has thus been made dramatically necessary. It is striking that the style of Mercy's two long speeches (839–58 and 879–98) is mainly sober, clear and explanatory, rather than aureate, ample and rhetorical. He offers to Mankind the example of Christ's teaching of the woman taken in adultery:

> He seyde to here theis wordys: 'Go and syn no more.'
> So to yow, go and syn no more.
>
> (851–2)

and draws from it clear instruction:

> If ye fele yoursylfe trappyd in the snare of your gostly enmy,
> Aske mercy anon.
>
> (855–6)

It is Mankind whose words are now elaborate and aureate, and the effect is not just that Mankind has returned to a state of grace, but also that elaborate speech is a symbol of those rich, wide spaces of the life of the spirit, which contrast with the barren littleness of the world and the body. The language, though excessive to modern ears at moments, conveys a sense of the luxuriant curlicues of life, a sort of baroque exuberance, by which Mankind's recovery is signalled.[14] Plain utterance is ingeniously mixed with decorated, so that the love of mercy is expressed in the manner of a courtly lyric, while Mercy simultaneously conveys explanation and warning to Mankind. The significance of the earlier actions in the play is pointed out succinctly:

Ye have thre adversaryis and he ys mayster of hem all:
That ys to say, the Dewell, the World, the Flesch and the Fell.
The New Gyse, Nowadayis, Nowgth, the World we may hem call;
And propyrly Titivillus syngnyfyth the Fend of helle;
The Flesch, that ys the unclene concupissens of your body.
These be your thre gostly enmyis, in whom ye hawe put your confidens.

(883–8)

The three enemies are figures met many times in the early moral drama
but the explanation here identifies one aspect of what has been unusual in
the play – that Mankind himself has included one element in the allegorical trio, the weakness of the flesh, and it is this which the Devil and the
World have exploited.

Your body ys your enmy; let hym not have hys wyll.

(897)

Mercy resumes the mantle of preacher to end the play, as he began it,
with an address to the audience. He puts on his learned rhetorical
language, too, but the speech is brief, and it does effectively communicate
the relationship between the needs of different dramatic moments. So, he
refers to his own role as follows:

Mankynd ys deliveryd by my faverall patrocynye.

(904)

One finds his earlier, simple statement of the same truth far more
memorable:

Remembyr how redy I was to help yow.

(891)

Yet, one can see a kind of appropriateness in the shift. We move from the
literal experience to the tropological significance visible in the etymologic-
al sense of the Latinate words: Mercy's help was an exercise of the grace
and favour of God and a fulfilment of his duty of fatherly care. In the
elevated words, we are shown that he has been true to his allegorical
nature; as he says 'I have do my propirte' ('performed my office').

I hope that it is clear from my comments on the different scenes that I
think *Mankind* is a clever play. It is, of the early allegorical dramas, the one
that most inventively turns the pattern of Innocence – Sin – Repentance
into a stage enactment of the states and conditions of being which this
pattern involves. It has been accused of neglecting the homiletic purpose
because it often leaves words and actions to make their own point.
Because it so vigorously and vividly presents words and actions which
illustrate worldly idleness, it has been accused of pandering to the very
tastes which it ruthlessly exposes. Though one can see in it much

evidence of its origins, it uses its material intelligently and transforms the common-places of homily into what makes sense in terms of drama. It is no criticism of *Mankind* to say that it is entertaining. It is a measure of the dramatist's success that he has created a stage comedy out of a homiletic idea, not a measure of failure. He has found ways of being irreverently satirical and yet of retaining the serious exemplary character of moral comedy, which goes through the confusions of experience to the peace of a recovery of mental security. These two aspects of comedy, *exemplum* and satire, are the two literary ideas which connect *Mankind* with other plays and writings of the period.

2.   *Exemplum-books and Exemplum-plays*

The primary sense of *exemplum* as a medieval literary term is that of a narrative inserted into a sermon to provide illustration of the point and to add variety for the congregation. The didactic justification for the use of tales was that precept was more forceful if proved by experience. The rhetorical justification, more open to objection, was that people would pay more attention to preaching if it was enlivened by anecdote: as Chaucer's Pardoner put it:

> Then telle I hem ensamples may oon
> Of olde stories, long tyme agoon;
> For lewed peple loven tales olde;
> Swich thinges can they wel reporte and holde.[15]

The use of moralised anecdotes in sermon literature has too long a history for me to summarise. It will have to suffice to say that the preaching friars made much use of narrative in their creation of a style of humane, popular homily, that the more austere commentators on preaching, such as Wycliffe, condemned the use of illustrative tales, because they diverted attention from doctrine and concentration on true understanding of Scripture, and that many fourteenth and fifteenth-century sermons and treatises are full of exemplary tales, drawn from a wide variety of sources, ancient and modern. To aid the preacher, collections of exempla were made and this type of collection became a literary form in its own right, the encyclopaedic collection of short stories with moral attached, such as the *Gesta Romanorum*.[16] Even larger was the early fifteenth-century collection of the fruits of the preacher's art in the previous three centuries made by the Dominican, John Bromyard, the *Summa Praedicantium*. Exempla were particularly useful to the compiler of handbooks of sins, since there was an even greater need to diversify literary effect in the compendium of sin than in a sermon. Several works belonging to both traditions (collections of exempla and surveys of sin) were translated into English in the fifteenth-century. The moral plays were composed during a period in which there were many other forms of literature treating moral themes.

To the student of medieval literature exempla are interesting not only in themselves, but also because, among other reasons, they provided source-material for many writers, they established the tale-collection as a literary form, and the relationship between narrative and moral message is a basic area of literary inquiry. The two most interesting literary uses of exempla in fourteenth-century English literature (as opposed, that is, to functional, homiletic uses) are in the two famous tale-collections of the period, Gower's *Confessio Amantis* and Chaucer's *The Canterbury Tales*. Gower's survey of love is based on the idea of the manual of sins, in which each sin (and its sub-types) is dealt with by means of explanation and illustrative story. Gower has never been given enough credit for the detailed analysis and sensitive representation of feeling which he achieved through the combination of the lover's confession (as he is catechised by the priest Genius) and the clearly expressed, well-shaped tales. As a poet he lacks Chaucer's robust imagination and flexibility of style, but he shows that stories do give life to moral ideas, and can act as images, through which theories may be experienced and retained in the mind.[17] In *The Canterbury Tales* Chaucer experimented with several types of exemplifying narrative,[18] but the one closest to the moral plays is *The Pardoner's Tale*. Here Chaucer uses the sermon and exemplum as yet another literary form for his virtuoso attentions, and, at the same time, creates an ironic portrait of a preacher whose sole aim in preaching is his own financial gain: the text for the Pardoner's sermon, *Radix malorum est cupiditas*, is thus exemplified both within and without the tale that follows. This story is the one about the three young louts who seek Death, but are diverted from thoughts of vengeance into avarice, by finding Death in the form of a heap of gold, through greed for which they kill each other. This could be the narrative outline for a moral play, and there is much within the outline that comes close to the themes and picture of life that the playwrights presented: the exhortation to avoid gluttony, swearing, idleness and all the life of the sordid world, the condemnation of pandering to fleshly appetite, the tavern-scene and the life of riot and vanity which the young men lead, the instances of irreverence, folly, envy, and, above all, the working out of retribution and the powerful figure of the strange old man who shows them the way to Death. The figures are not personifications, but, in a different sense, they are allegorical. The three rioters, ancestors of New Guise, Nowadays and Nought, embody the follies and crimes of vicious youth, while the old man speaks for the weariness of age, longing for, but unable to find kindly death to release him.[19] The economy and suggestive power of Chaucer's treatment of moral ideas provides a standard by which one can judge fifteenth-century moral plays, not often to their advantage.

If *The Pardoner's Tale* shows the imaginative possibilities of the exemplum, it is in the hand-books of sin that one finds the actual tradition upon which *Mankind* and other moral plays drew. Coogan and others have shown that a possible source for *Mankind* was the fifteenth-century allegorical treatise *Jacob's Well*, which was well described many years ago, by its editor, as one of 'that numerous class of manuals, in prose and verse, whose object it was to condense the whole penitential lore of the time into a code for the use of laymen or clerical persons'.[20] Other well-known examples of the type are the *Ayenbite of Inwit*, *The Pricke of Conscience*, *Handlyng Synne* and Chaucer's *Parson's Tale* (most of which are endebted to Friar Laurence's *Somme des Vices et des Vertus*). In *Jacob's Well* teaching is threaded through with stories, taken from several sources, including Jacques de Vitry, the *Vitae Patrum* and the *Legenda Aurea*. The sections on idleness show the traditional nature of the attitudes and ideas in *Mankind*. The tract teaches the reader to do good works so that 'the feend may fynde thee occupyed', and illustrates different kinds of idleness and negligence, such as too great an interest in sports and pastimes:

> Idelnes is also whanne, oute of tyme & out of mesure, thou yevyst the to huntyng, hawkyng, foulyng, fyschinge; to gon to wakys & to wrestlynges, to daunsynges & to steraclys, to tavernys, to revell, to ryott, to schetinges, to feyrys, to markettys on the holy-days, & to chaffarynge, & levyst thi paryschcherche & thi servyse; & in doinge thi pylgrimage on holy dayis; & in pleying at the two hande swerd, at swerd & bokelere, & at two pyked staf, at the hurlebatte; & to harpyn, lutyn, to scornyn, & to yevyn the to evyll cumpany, in mys-spendyng thi good & thi frendys good, & in yevyying evyl exaumple, & in wykked desyres in evyll wyllys, & in steryng othere to evyll, in wycked counseylyng, in defoulyng the halyday, in synne & in evyll werkys.[21]

The teaching is illustrated not only by instances, but also by images:

> Slowthe makyth the the restyng place of the devyl, for thou art the feendys pylwe. Slowthe makyth the as a cyte unwallyd, redy & esy for alle feendys to entryn into thi soule. Slowthe makyth the as a schetyng hyll, redy to be schett wyth the arwe of every temptacyoun.[22]

And, finally, it is illustrated by anecdotes, such as the story from Jacques de Vitry of the demon who gathers over-skipped words from religious verses in a sack and writes idle words spoken in church on a scroll. It is this fiend who is called, in other texts, Tutivillus, and who is the origin of the Devil in *Mankind*. Several scholars have argued that the playwright borrowed him from the sin-manual because of Titivillus' association with idleness of speech, which becomes a main theme in the play. When the author of *Jacob's Well* returns to the subject of vain thoughts, words and deeds in chapter 37, he repeats the story of the demon with the scroll, after emphasising the wickedness of idle words. (He quotes Matthew, as does *Mankind*: 'of every ydel woord thou spekyst, thou shalt gyve accountys at the day of Dome'.). He then adds two other demonic tales, one of a young sinner tempted by fiends, and another of a fiend who takes Abbot Macarius to watch the antics of his colleagues:

> The feend seyde 'Abbot, come & see what we do!' The abbott wente into the chirche, & see ovyr-all in the chirche dyverse feendys smal as chylderyn, blewe as men of Inde, renynge al abowte in the cherche, & scornyng there every man, makyng a mowe, & puttynge here fyngerys to the eyyen of summe, and thei sleptyn, & whenne thei awokyn the feendys grecyd here lyppes wyth here oynementys in here box, & thanne the folk iangelyd, & telde talys.[23]

Whether or not the author of *Mankind* drew on *Jacob's Well*, one can not but see the general resemblance between the sort of illustration found in such a manual and the moral basis of the play. The story of Mankind's resolve to eschew idleness by tilling the soil and the tricks, unsuccessful and successful, used by the Devil and his subordinate vices to subvert that resolve is an illustrative tale placed between the homiletic opening, which establishes the contrary states of virtue and sin, and the repentant and explanatory close. As Siegfried Wenzel points out, the psychology follows the treatment of sloth in the manuals.[24] Mankind is tempted and tricked into letting bodily hardship make good work tedious; he gives in to sleep and becomes a prey to the Devil and is led eventually to the culmination of *accidie*, suicidal despair. The roles of New Guise, Nowadays, and Nought stem from the activities of demons, such as are described in *Jacob's Well*; they can also be seen as servants of Dame Idleness, as she is described in Lydgate's *Pilgrimage of the Life of Man* and elsewhere.[25]

Another treatise which shows similar exemplary illustration of the sin of sloth is the famous survey of sin, Robert Manning's *Handlyng Synne*.[26] Manning's treatment of sloth also features demons, particularly the devil Terlyncel (meaning 'Draw-sheet'), whose function is to make men too sleepy on Sundays to get up to go to Mass. More turn up in the narrative of an English squire who puts off repentance until too late, and who is shown his sins written in a great book carried by two black devils, 'foule stynkyng/Wyth glesyng yyen and mouthe grennyng'. An interesting possibility, which I have explored elsewhere, is that the author of *Mankind* knew the mid-fifteenth-century instruction-book Peter Idley's *Instructions to his Son*, which uses *Handlyng Synne* as the main source of Book II (together with Lydgate's *The Fall of Princes*).[27] Idley fuses together Manning's demon Terlyncel and the other activities of aspects of sloth to create a general slothful devil (under the name Treselincellis), who creates a whole *ambience* of idleness:

> And if a freer com Goddis wordis to preche,
> Expownyng holy writte or of seyntis lyves,
> Than into a corner prevely woll he reche
> And talke with maydenes and mennes wyffis,

> Pleye with her purces, keyes and knyves.
> He is a speciall servannt to Treselincellis the feende;
> It is to feare at last myscheif woll be thende.[28]

Here, in little, we have the figures of the preaching friar, Mercy, the slothful demon, mankind turned into the devil's servant and mischief as the result – a thumbnail sketch of the plot of *Mankind*. Idley's expression of the traditional ideas of idleness is often suggestive of the moral plays, as, for instance:

> Then woll the feende put in his thought
> That all worldlie thyng was made for man.[29]

Idley too, stresses the aspect of sloth which provides the material of the last part of the play, obstinacy in sin.

I hope I have said enough to indicate that the thinking in the play is rooted in the traditional matter of these works of Christian didacticism, which enliven teaching by continual illustration – not only stories, but also brief imagined situations, the legends of demons, comparisons, images and allegories. Two features are of main importance: first, the sense of the exemplum as forming the central part of a didactic demonstration, and, secondly, the treatment of sin in the manuals under the headings of the Seven Deadly Sins. I think of *Mankind* as an exemplum in both respects. Its actions form an illustration of the workings of sloth, and the play consists of the three necessary stages; theoretical exposition, anecdotal illustration, explanation with reinforcement of the message. Secondly, the fact that one can identify the play as an illustration of sloth (despite the general references to the World, Flesh and Devil and the implications of all kinds of sin) shows it to belong to the tradition, associated with the idea of the Paternoster play, of separating evil out into its types.

There are clear signs of the didactic ancestry of *Mankind*, and of some other plays, in their beginning and ending in homily. The life of such plays tends to be in the illustrations of sin, but they needed the framework of sermon to provide a statement of theme and a conclusion, and to make them complete units in artistic as well as moral terms. It was difficult to make the homiletic parts of such a play dramatically telling, and development, which is already to be seen in *Mankind*, had to be towards greater dependence on *showing* the results of experience, rather than on mere assertion. Hence the plays which are essentially illustrations (of sin, of a moral point, and of the nature of the world) tend towards the inclusion of more instances of conduct. This is a movement towards various kinds of comedy – using the word in its widest sense of a drama that ends in continuation and in profiting from experience.

The basic pattern of the kind of drama which may be recognised as an exemplum-play is a sequence of three stages: a homiletic or theoretical beginning, an anecdote of sin, and a concluding judgment or message. However, one can recognise the exemplum-play in a variety of forms. It can be allegorical, as in *Mankind*, where the illustrative 'a man' has become an actual personification. It can be literal, but use general, anonymous figures. It can be Scriptural and historical.

One version may be seen in Pageant 24 of the N-Town cycle, *The Woman taken in Adultery*. Here, the opening speech of Jesus (five 8-line stanzas) provides the homiletic framework. He begins:

> Man, for thi synne take repentaunce.

He preaches mercy, speaks of his role as redeemer, and pleads:

> Love me ageyn, I aske no more,
> Thow thou mys-happe and synne ful sore,
> Yit turne agen and mercy crave.
>
> (20–2)

In the fourth stanza he bids:

> Vppon thi neybore be not vengabyl
>
> (25)

and in the fifth:

> Eche man to othyr be mercyable,
> And mercy he xal have at nede.
>
> (33–4)

Each of these threads in the speech is the starting-point for an element in the story which follows. The figures in the story are anonymous representatives of attitudes and conduct, identified as Scribe, Pharisee, Accuser, Young Man and Woman. The first three are enemies of Christ; they share one of the functions usually given to the Vices in moral drama, that of plotting against good. It is their intention to discredit Jesus by forcing him to support the legal punishment (death) for an adulterous whore caught in the act, and thus to contradict his preaching of mercy. Their role as lying intriguers is re-inforced by their hypocrisy, as they call on Jesus 'To gyff trewe dom and just sentence' in apparent zeal for law:

> So we have brought here to your presens,
> Becaws ye ben a wyse prophete,
> That ye xal telle be consyens
> What deth to hyre ye thynke most mete.
>
> (197–200)

Such illustration of disingenuous deceit is a more significant kind of 'realism' than the touch of actual life in the famous stage direction which has the young man running off with his breeches in his hand, when Scribe, Pharisee and Accuser burst in upon him and the woman. In contrast to the malicious accusers, the sinner herself is presented with sympathy and pathos, first as someone violently attacked, whose pleas are rejected and who is reviled, and then as a penitent. The classic three-part design is completed by Jesus' delivery of judgment, his writing on the ground the sins of the accusers, and, after they have fled, his teaching of the Woman:

> Loke that thou leve in honeste.
> (278)

This turns easily into an address to the audience.

> Whan man is contrite and hath wonne grace,
> God wele not kepe olde wreth in mynde.
> (289–90)

The pageant thus tells a moral anecdote which acts as an illustration of the sin of Lechery as well as of the teaching of Jesus on the theme of mercy to the repentant. The tale shows the turning again of the sinner and the discomfiture of those who are 'vengabyl' and lack mercy. The sand-wiching of the exemplum between the bread of Jesus' teaching provides a strong, clear structure, which makes it one of the most formally effective pageants in the cycles. The playwright adds to this a simple directness in the expression of feeling, as in the Woman's repentance:

> With all myn hert I am sory.
> (264)

and neat touches of comic exposure, both of the young man and the accusers. The result is a strong acting-out of Christian ideas. The pageant demonstrates one solution to the problem of creating plays out of lessons, which is to use Jesus simultaneously as teacher and as hero. His voice delivers the moral lesson at the beginning and at the end, and his actions within the story demonstrate the lesson. At the same time he is threatened by the plotters against him, and his judgment of the Woman becomes a triumphant defeat of malice, as well as exemplification of Christian mercy.

A different solution is to avoid the role of preacher and the danger of undigested lumps of didactic matter by absorbing the element of homily in the exemplum-play into dramatic situations. This may result in an apparent (or even a real) reduction of the moral force of the play. This process is, to my mind, what one can see in the Towneley *Second Shepherd's Play*. The basic three-part structure of moral introduction, exemplary narrative and resolution in Christian hope and love is visible, but the relationship of the parts is oblique, not explicit. The first stage is in the form of a trio of complaints from the three shepherds, who lament in turn the evils and misfortunes of the world. Their speeches mingle together homiletic assertions of the mutability of the world and satirical complaints against contemporary social injustices, especially those caused by maintenance and purveyance. The Wakefield Master's dramatisation of the voice of the working man complaining of his hard lot is one of his many touches designed to bring scriptural matters close to his audience. It has the function of giving a local habitation and a name to the burden of the medieval *Contemptus Mundi* tradition; the naturalistic surface gives particularity, but beneath one sees the traditional idea that the acts of man are all manifestations of the vanity of the world. It is a theme of the play that earthly life is out of joint and in need of the order and meaning given by the Redemption. The evils of the world are illustrated, amusingly and suggestively, by the anecdote of Mak the thief. As in *The Woman taken in Adultery*, the moral conclusion is reached through the exposure of crime and judgment of it. Of course the version here is more intriguing, because of the folk-play quality in the figures of Mak and Gyll and the fun of the disguising of the sheep as a babe in the cradle, with its teasing suggestions of a devilish, anti-Christian nativity. But if one looks at the pageant in the context of exemplum-plays in general, one notices other things. Mak first enters disguised, by both a gentleman's dress and a southern accent, and one recognises this as a typical devil's trick, as is his later casting of a spell upon the sleeping shepherds. (Compare Titivillus' treatment of the hero in *Mankind*.) The story is an anecdote of covetousness, which both illustrates the shepherds' opening complaints of injustice and hardship and prepares for the lesson of the nativity which comes at the end. The story is one of taking and concealing; the final scene is based on revealing and giving. The nearest to sermon in the pageant is the transition between the second and third stages (Gabriel's appearance to the shepherds and their recalling of the prophecies of Christ's coming); here is the revelation. The pageant ends in the presentation of gifts and in blessing. The playwright again shows his skill in weaving together naturalistic touches, in the gifts of the shepherds, and doctrinal significance, as the paradoxes of Christ as baby and conqueror, as newly-made and maker, are expressed in the shepherds' antiphonal chants of greeting to the Christ-child.

In this pageant the roles of Devil and man and the expression of Christian truth are more dispersed than is the case in allegorical drama. Mak has enough of the Devil about him to show his kinship with Titivillus and others, and crime, deceit and humour are a characteristically vicious combination, but in him Devil, Vice and the average sinner-in-the-street come together. He turns into hen-pecked husband and cheeky comic turn, before eventually, if briefly, becoming the repentant sinner. So the role of mankind is shared between the sinful Mak and the three innocent shepherds. The latter move through the three stages common to mankind-figures in the moral plays (innocence, experience of the evils of the world and understanding), but they are scriptural figures with a particular part to play in unfolding the story of the Nativity, and this controls the nature of their fulfilment of the role of man. They represent an ordinariness of reaction, first to the vicissitudes of fortune, then to their loss, the discovery and punishment of Mak, and finally to the coming of the Saviour, but their roles are subordinate to the matter, and in the last part they are used simply as a trio of voices to express prophecy and praise. The authoritative voice of Christian truth, shared among the shepherds in their phase as Chorus, the angel and Mary, is delayed unusually long in this pageant. To some the ingenuity of the Wakefield master has defeated its object, and produced a secular comedy in which religious revelation becomes an after-thought. It is certainly not typical of the cycle-pageants. It has been influenced by the non-scriptural drama and has become a play separable from its context, a play in three acts or stages (showing its connections with the form of the demonstrative moral play). Seen as an exemplum-play, it seems particularly effective; its exemplary force is clear but expressed indirectly, through a succession of motifs and moods, with the comedy of deceit and dispute eventually resolved in giving, harmony and blessed joy.

Both *The Woman taken in Adultery* and the *Second Shepherds' Play* are examples of stories of sinners which illustrate or embellish Christian teaching. A different idea of the exemplum-play resulted when important figures in the New Testament narrative were treated in such a way as to place them in exemplary roles. The stories of Herod, Pilate and Judas, as I have said earlier, are treated in some plays as exemplifications of the punishment of pride, the torture of guilt, and so on. The 'comic' idea of exemplum is found when wickedness is overcome and innocence is proved. An interesting example of this type of play is Pageant 14 of the N-Town cycle, *The Trial of Joseph and Mary*.

This is a well-constructed play, consisting of a Prologue, three main scenes or phases and an epilogue; it deals with the Apocryphal story that Mary and Joseph had taken vows of virginity, and, when Mary was known to be pregnant, were tried, Joseph for breaking his vow and Mary for adultery, and required to prove their innocence by drinking a bitter draught, the drink of vengeance, which would disfigure or harm them if guilty. The story was told by Lydgate in his *Life of our Lady* and this (rather than Continental plays, which do not include the theme) is the probable source of the dramatist's interest in the subject.[30] He treats it with verve and originality.

The 32-line Prologue is a call by a Summoner to attend the ecclesiastical court for the trial; this places the action of the play at once in the world of fabliau or Langland's tavern:

> I warne yow here all abowte
> That I somown yow all the rowte!

> Loke ye feyl for no dowte
> > at the court to pere!
> Both Johan Jurdon and Geoffrey Gyle,
> Malkyn Mylkedoke, and fayr Mabyle,
> Stevyn Sturdy and Jake-at-the-style
> > and Sawdyr Sadelere.
> > > (5–12)

The roll-call of proper names, mingling allegorical names with comic low-life ones, continues with a few touches of familiar satire at the expense of church-courts:

> Cok Crane and Davy Drydust,
> Luce Lyere and Letyce Little-Trust,
> Miles the Miller and Colle Crack-Crust,
> > Bothe Bette the Baker and Robyn Rede.
> And loke ye rynge wele in your purs,
> For ellys your cawse may spede the wurs,
> Thow that ye slynge Goddys curs
> > Even at myn hede. Fast com away!
> > > (21–8)

The satirical tradition drawn on in the invention of the summoner sets the tone, and the dramatist moves easily into an opening scene between two detractors, who first establish their allegorical nature (they are Raise-slander and Backbiter) and then set about Joseph and Mary:

> *2nd Det.* Ya, that old shrewe Joseph, my trouth I plyght,
> > Was so anameryd upon that mayd
> > That of hyre bewte when he had syght
> > He sesyd net tyll had here asayd.
>
> *1st Det.* A, nay, nay! Wel wers she hath hym payd.
> > Sum fresch yonge galaunt she loveth wel more
> > That his leggys to here hath leyd,
> > And that doth greve the old man more.
> > > (49–56)

The two slanderers, delighting in malicious gossip, present their case to the Bishop (Mary's kinsman) and two Doctors of Law in session, who are reluctant to believe such shame 'of that good virgyn, fayr maid Mary', and who reprove the detractors. ('Ye be to besy of your langage.') However, they agree that the case must be heard. In the middle section the summoner goes to Mary and Joseph and brings them to court, and the third section is the trial, in which Mary and Joseph in turn are accused, defend themselves, take the drink of vengeance and go seven times round the altar, come through the ordeal unscathed, and are declared innocent. The first detractor is made to follow their example and falls in pain, crying:

> Owt! Owt! Alas, what heylith my sculle?
> A! myn heed with fyre me thynkyth is brent!
> Mercy, good Mary! I do me repent
> Of my cursyd and fals langage.
>
> (331–4)

The end of the story is given to Mary and Joseph who thank God in an epilogue to the action:

> Honouryd in hevyn be that hygh Lord,
> Whos endles grace is so habundant
> That he doth showe the trewe record
> Of the wyghte that is his trewe servaunt.
>
> (361–4)

Here then is another version of the pattern of the exemplum-play. It is an illustration both of the sin of Envy, from enactment to punishment and repentance, and of innocence, from false accusation to trial and vindication. Though the dramatist is dealing with the historical figures of Mary and Joseph, he has turned the episode into an allegorical antithesis between good and evil, mainly through the familiar dramatic device of a trial-scene. In this scene he makes an effective contrast between the language of the two sides; the simplicity of Mary and Joseph is enhanced into truth and dignity by the insults and lewd familiarity of the detractors, whose speeches belong to the dramatic tradition of Devil and Vice in their combination of malice and a gleeful, racy idiom:

> Now, sere, evyl thedom come to thi snowte!
> What heylygth thi leggys now to be lame?
> Thow dedyst hem put ryght freschly owte
> Whan thow dedyst play with yon yonge dame!
>
> (229–32)

The setting of a medieval church-court and the figures of the Summoner and the Doctors are in the anachronistic vein of many medieval treatments of Scripture, but particularly close to the Wakefield Master's treatment of the trial of Jesus before Caiaphas and Annas. But more striking than the effect of contemporary realism is the way in which the play succeeds in dramatising innocence, a passive quality which can only make a positive impact when it is attacked and has to prove itself. In order to prove it here, the dramatist has created images of the world and has recourse to satirical caricatures of sinful behaviour, such as are found in sketches of gossips and backbiters in the *Ancrene Wisse* and other instruction-books about sin; by this means evil may be turned into active beings.

At the same time the use of the magic test of innocence brings the action into the world of miracle, such as is found not only in saints' lives but also in many romances about the preservation of innocence such as *Athelston* and Chaucer's *Man of Law's Tale.* So the action begins in the realistic, racy fabliau manner of the Summoner and the Detractors, but brings this into contact with a different level of being, that of mystery, romance and miracle.

The treatment of Scripture in this play turns the innocence of Joseph and Mary into an act of exemplification culminating (as in the other plays I have discussed) in an act of judgment, and rounded off with gratitude for the justice of God. Only the first stage of the play lacks a homiletic ring: it functions as preparation for the exemplary trial-scene by establishing worldly judgment as seeing always the worst. (The effect draws on the earlier dramatisation, particularly vivid in the N-Town cycle, of Joseph's own suspicions of Mary.) We thus begin with the voices which, in the course of the play, are to be proved wrong and to be rejected, rather than, as is more usual, the voices which are to be proved right. This, as with the *Second Shepherd's Play*, shows an intelligent absorption of homiletic ideas into dramatic situations.

As a last type of exemplum-play I put forward a more dubious case, the fragment of a play known as *Dux Moraud*.[31] All that survives of this is the actor's part of Duke Moraud himself, written on a strip cut from a fourteenth-century legal roll in mid-fifteenth century, and written in a dialect most closely resembling a collection of poems from Bury St Edmunds. The fragment shows another facet of the variety of East Anglian drama in this period. Duke Moraud was the dominant male character in a story of incest and murder, and as bad a villain as ever trod boards. He not only, during his wife's absence, persuaded his daughter to become his mistress, but incited her to murder first her mother and then the child of the incestuous union. In an English poem which tells a version of the tale, the father's repentance and death, at his daughter's hands, end the first half of the poem;[32] this is followed by a second half dealing with the subsequent fate of the daughter, who leaves the country, lives as a prostitute, but repents, dies and is forgiven. In outline this sounds as if medieval drama had made a sudden leap into the world of Webster, Ford and Middleton, and some historians of drama have identified *Dux Moraud* as a kind of half-submerged rock in the uncharted seas of medieval secular drama. But it seems more likely that, if we had the whole play, it would be seen to belong to the exemplum tradition. The sort of romance from which the play is derived tends to be a seedy mixture of sexual sensationalism and piety.[33] The slander of a virtuous young heroine is a major theme in homiletic romance literature; the rarer version in which the heroine is actually corrupted and drawn into sin is one which brings romance into the Magdalene pattern of sin and repentance (a subject dealt with in the Digby play of *Mary Magdalene*, to be discussed in a later chapter).

The part of the Duke indicates a rather crude treatment of the course of repentance; its interest is that it is presented through an individual, fictional figure rather than an allegorical one. In excellent spirits, he expresses himself in an exuberant alliterative verse, similar to *The Castle of Perseverance*:

> I am myhtful and mery markyd in mynd,
> I am flour fayrest be fryt for to fare,
> I am fayrest in fas, ferly to fynd,
> I am loveliche in lond, lyttest in lare,
> I am comely and curteys, and crafty of kynd.
>
> (164–8)

A moment later he hears a church bell and in the next speech the moral reversal has taken place:

> A synful kaytyf I am,
> Synfully I ave wrowt blam
>   Be gret tyme of my lyfe.
> Now, Cryst, ase thou me bowt,
> Forgeve me that blam that I ave wrowt,
>   And mak me sumquat blythe!
>
> (183–8)

At the end he dies in piety:

> *In manus tuas, domine!*
> Jhesu have mercy on me,
>   And save my sowle fro helle.
>
> (266–8)

The speeches and the staccato shifts they seem to indicate do not suggest that there was any subtlety or psychological realism in the treatment, but the exemplary course of the story is clear enough.

Here is another link in the chain which I suggest stretches from the Paternoster Plays through the fifteenth century. The tradition was one of illustration of sins, or the classification of Scriptural and Apocryphal incidents as exemplary of particular areas of sin and virtue. *Dux Moraud* was an illustration of a particular type of Lechery, *Mankind* of Sloth and in other plays Pride, Covetousness and Envy provide the theme which the story exemplifies. Concentration on an individual story and a particular sin produces a type of play which is a moral episode, rather than a whole-scale dramatisation of the battle between virtue and vice. The exemplary episode is quite a different type of play from the panoramic, epic play such as *The Castle of Perseverance*, despite the occurrence of common ideas. The illustrative lesson, which is learned for the rest of life, or the proof of innocence and the reformation of guilt are essentially 'comic' ideas, in that they lead from moral confusion to the establishment of some sort of order or re-assertion of moral and social law. Many of the exemplary plays are also comic in the more general sense, and this is partly the result of the use of satire, which I have mentioned in passing in a number of plays just discussed, and which is an especially important element in *Mankind* itself.

3. *Medieval Satire*

Fourteenth and fifteenth-century satire, an important but neglected[34] aspect of medieval English literature, draws on three main traditions: a tradition, found in sermons and instruction-books, of exposure of vice and folly in the condemning voice of the preacher; a tradition, found in lyrics, of scornful attacks on contemporary political and social trends; and a tradition of literary satire, derived distantly from Horace and Juvenal, which had developed in later hands into set themes, such as the follies of women and the vices of different classes in society, and set forms, such as the dramatic monologue and the satirical portrait. The traditions often overlap in practice and it is difficult to separate one strand from another, but differences do manifest themselves in actual examples of satirical writing. In Chaucer's best-known piece of satire, the *General Prologue* to *The Canterbury Tales*, he uses portraits of (supposed) individuals to create a detailed, realistic impression of a group. The pictures accumulate into a view of society, since one sees that the group includes representatives of the church, of women, of aristocracy and bourgeoisie, and so on. Chaucer is drawing on the medieval Latin tradition of estates satire, in which the moral failings of Nobles, Church and Commons are exposed, but, as Jill Mann has ably demonstrated, in using the class framework without the explicit didacticism, Chaucer has produced a subtler form of satire that works by the juxtaposition of ideal and deficient representatives of class, of office and of religion.[35]

In *The Parson's Tale* one can see Chaucer working in a different tradition. Here the framework is that of the Seven Deadly Sins and the satire is of the scathing variety whose purpose is simply to illustrate folly and vice. Much of it consists of invective and abuse, but it produces flourishes of the grotesque which take it into the realms of satire, as in the following section on the vanity of clothing (part of the castigation of Pride):

> To speken of the horrible disordinat scantnesse of clothyng, as been thise kutted sloppes, or heynselyns, that thurgh hire shortnesse ne covere nat the shameful membres of man, to wikked entente. Alles! somme of hem showen

the boce of hir shap, and the horrible swollen membres, that semeth lik the maladie of hirnia, in the wrappynge of hir hoses; and eek the buttokes of hem faren as it were the hyndre part of a she-ape in the fulle of the moone.[36]

This is a characteristic product of the sermon tradition. Langland's pictures of sin, particularly in the Prologue and the first five passus of the B-Text of *Piers Plowman* show observation of the weaknesses and follies of human society translated into moral allegory. In the Field full of Folk, the scenes with Lady Meed and the confessions of the Sins, Langland creates a succession of panoramas of everyday sin and absurdity. The poet's transforming imagination makes the figures and the words unique, but the material is recognisable as that of a sermon tradition of attacks on ignorant and neglectful clerics, on the clergy's greed for profitable livings and on others whose lives are motivated by covetousness, especially lawyers, merchants, friars and members of other religious communities.[37]

In the lyrics one finds a tradition of lampoon and journalistic comment, mainly along the lines that everything is going to the dogs; the instability of things, the follies of fashion and the failings of women are favourite topics. In many such lyrics the specific impulse of the poem merges into general abuse of folly and complaint of the evils of the age:[38] for instance, the particular political events which perhaps stimulated the poet to write 'The Bisson Leads the Blind' have almost disappeared into the familiar motif of reversal ('Truthe ys turned to trechery', 'holy chyrche ys chaf-fare', etc.).[39] However, general themes can turn up in new guises, as fifteenth-century poems about over-dressed braggarts, or 'gallants' show. They are part of the general exposure of pride and the vanity of dress, already seen in *The Parson's Tale*, but express specific contemporary criticism too. There is some individual bite, for example, in the poem in MS Rawlinson poet. 34, as well as one or two reminders of *Mankind*:

> Galaunt, by thy gyrdyl ther hangyth a purss;
> Ther-in ys neyther peny nor crosse,
> But iii dysse, and crystys curse –
>   Huff, a galawnt!
> Galaunt, with thy dagger a crosse
> And thy hanggyng pouche upon thy narse,
> Thow art ful abyl to stele a horse,
>   Huff, a Galauntt![40]

Between this kind of 'satire' of abuses of the age, together with that of *The Parson's Tale* and *Piers Plowman* on the one hand, and, on the other, the satire in Chaucer's *General Prologue* John Peter makes a fundamental distinction, seeing the latter as 'satire' in the tradition, coming from Juvenal, of realistic immediacy and sharp individuality, while the former works are examples of 'complaint', a broader, more impersonal and abstract writing, lacking the sharpness, agility and precision of satire. The Complaint, as Peter sees it, 'is usually conceptual, and often allegorical';[41]

examples of it, such as the influential twelfth-century poem of Bernard of Cluny, *De Contemptu Mundi*, and many sermons, devote their energies to attacking (in the words of the Catechism) 'the pomps and vanity of this wicked world and all the sinful lusts of the flesh'. Peter sums up by saying:

> To put all the examples of Complaint together – the diatribes, the lamentations, the verse homilies, the moral poems and fables, 'Mirror' and *Timor Mortis* poems – is only to reconstruct, in a versified form, the thunderings of the preachers.[42]

Peter's distinction is useful, but the question of whether something is 'complaint' or 'satire' often becomes a matter of judging literary effectiveness rather than literary kind. In many examples of medieval satire one finds simply attack (from reasoned criticism to raving abuse), but sometimes one finds, either in a few passages or, occasionally, in a whole work, a comic exaggeration or a witty twist which takes one beyond complaint into a more imaginative experience where laughter is harnessed to moral teaching.

In the drama there are passages of both complaint and satire, and there are a few whole plays which can fairly be seen as satirical. The form one meets most frequently is the complaint of the abuses of the age. The impulse is mainly the one ascribed as early as 1389 to the York Paternoster play, in which 'all manner of vices and sins were held up to scorn, and the virtues held up to praise'. The main subjects for criticism are the instability of the times (shown in the loss of the old values and the pursuit of money, position and power regardless of the traditional sanctities of social hierarchy, the duties of the church, the bonds of marriage etc.), and the vanity of the pursuit of fashion and worldly display. In *The Pride of Life* the original homiletic tone occurs in the Bishop's arraignment of the 'world nowadays':

> The world is nou so wo-lo-wo,
> In suc bal ibound,
> That dred of God is al ago.
> And treut is go to ground.
> (327–30)

The list of reversals is the main rhetorical device and the nearest to satirical 'wit' in such complaints, and even though it becomes a cliché, the turning of *love* into *lechery* and *truth* into *treachery* continues to have just a little edge of verbal magic because of the bringing together as a rhyme-pair two ideas originally apart.

The Wakefield Master uses the complaint of the world's uncertainty as an introduction to both of the Shepherds' Plays. In the first the themes are general:

> Thus this world, as I say, farys on ylk syde,
> For after oure play com sorows unryde,
> For he that most may, when he syttys in
> pryde,
> When it comes on assay is kesten down wyde.
> (Towneley, *Prima Pastorum* 10–13)

But in the second there is more precision and more kick, as the complaints flow into the channel of social protest at taxation and oppression by 'thyse gentlery man', especially the hangers-on of the rich who

> . . . can make purveance,
> With boste and bragance,
> And all is thrugh mantenance
> Of men that are gretter.
> Ther shal come a swane, as prowde as a po,
> He must borow my wane, my ploghe also;
> Then I am full fane to grawnt or he go!
> (Towneley, *Secunda Pastorum* 33–9)

The irony of the last line and the touches of scornful exaggeration give the catalogue of grievances a genuinely satirical smack.

In some plays the voice of the Devil is used as an ironical register of the world's sins; the demonic glee in evil gives a twist akin to Chaucer's apparent approval of the 'good' opinion of his monk, the 'pleasant' absolution of his friar, and so on. The recording demon Tutivillus in the Towneley *Judgment* enlivens the play with a fine roll-call of sinners, which gives a scornful picture of the way of the world:

> All harlottys and horres
> And bawdys that procures,
> To bryng thaym to lures,
>   Welcom to my see!
> Ye lurdanes and lyars, mychers and thefes,
> Flytors and flyars, that all men reprefes,
> Spolars, extorcyonars – Welcome, my lefes!
> Fals Jurars and usarars, to symony that clevys
>   To tell;
> Hasardars and dysars,
> Fals dedys forgars,
> Slanderars, back-bytars!
>   All unto hell!
> (355–67)

Death and the Last Judgment could become occasions of satire, because satire was used to redress social imbalance: so the idea that before Death or at the Judgment all would be equal was the trigger for an unsparing review of the failings of the rich and powerful. In the Towneley Play this joins with the effective theatrical device of characterising demons through energetic enjoyment of malice.

Another Devil (in the N-Town cycle) is given a splendid Prologue to the Passion Play. The Devil's boasts and his determination to outwit Christ lead to encouragement of the audience's wickedness. The Demon displays the luxurious finery of his dress to lure his hearers to vain thoughts and reckless extravagance, and to incite them to scorn of the poor and to lechery and pride. The reversal of virtue into vice here becomes a matter of hypocritical pretence:

> I have browth yow new namys, and wyl ye se why:
> For synne is so plesaunt to ech mannys intent.
> Ye xall kalle pride onesté, and naturall kind lechery,
> And covetyse wysdam, there tresure is present . . .   (109–12)

An alternative way of drawing satirical common-places into the Scriptural plays was to take the opportunities offered by particular areas of subject-matter. So, for instance, the Wakefield Master made use of satirical exaggeration of courtly language in his semi-comic treatment of Herod, whose mixture of ranting cruelty, French phrases such as 'ditizance doutance', and the occasional flourish of poetic ecstasy ('So light is my saull, That all of sugar is my gall'), creates a particularly nasty impression. Even more liable than aristocratic airs to set off a satirical pen were the never-failing deficiencies of women. Though Eve herself is not portrayed as a comic figure, she comes in for plenty of the traditional medieval anti-feminist satire; the comments of Satan and Adam display her as prototype of female folly and disobedience. Noah's wife and Pilate's wife, Dame Procula, are treated more freely and are presented, with various shades of humour and wit, as instances of obstinacy and disobedience on the one hand and woman's vanity in beauty, clothing and wits on the other. The Chester playwright characterises the knights in the *Massacre of the Innocents* with a few digs at chivalry's empty boasts. Other minor characters are used to introduce a note of irreverence and comic realism into plays: cheeky boys, phlegmatic Yorkshiremen, bold gossips, and so on, all have moments when a pungent comment humorously expresses a deflating truth.

One could, by going on adding moments and figures which have a satirical touch, accumulate a good body of evidence for the view that the satirical impulse was a major thread in fifteenth-century treatment of Scripture and morality. But, of course, in most plays it has a subordinate role, and is simply part of the mixture of ideas and effects. There are only a few plays in which satire is a major component, but the few suffice to show the development of satire in the period. At the end of the fifteenth and in the early sixteenth century satire became a more frequent and more central literary kind. Court life is presented bitingly by both Barclay and Skelton. New forms of satire from the Theocritan pastoral tradition enlarge the range of poetic expression, and one finds a stronger determination, in Skelton particularly, to present a view of the world as a place in which all men are either fools or knaves. The movement towards this may be seen in a number of plays before 1520: *Mankind*, the Towneley *Killing of Abel*, *Youth*, *Hick Scorner* and parts of *Magnificence* and *Nature*.

Whether one regards *Mankind* as a satirical play depends mainly on one's view of the three vices, New Guise, Nowadays and Nought. They have been described as crucial to the theatrical quality of the play because of their zest and lively malice, which resembles that given elsewhere to demons.[43] They are identified in the play as the World, but critics have not often been satisfied with that explanation alone. Cushman (and Bevington) saw them as part of the 'abbreviation of the Seven Deadly Sins', which led eventually to the concentration of evil in plays in one figure called 'the Vice'. Wenzel suggested that they were based on Langland's 'wastours', type-figures who represented idleness in the world and opposition to the 'wynneres', those who till the soil to provide sustenance. L. K. Stock has more recently argued that they are based on Job's false friends, who pretend to console but actually undermine.[44] Other possible source-figures are the three rioters in *The Pardoner's Tale*. They speak at times from among the audience and Southern's interest in their exact location at line 233ff. is not only a question of staging: are we meant to see them as speaking from among ourselves and therefore as representatives of our own worldly attitudes?[45]

In the play their identification with the World is not made explicit until the end. At the beginning their nature is in their names. Nought defines himself (269–76) partly by saying 'My name is Nought', which has the punning sense that his reputation is worthless as well as its literal meaning, and partly by displaying himself as a penniless ne'er-do-well, seeking empty pleasure in stale lust. The name of New Guise is the subject of explicit distinction by Mercy between 'the goode new gyse' and 'the vycyouse gyse'; obviously New Guise belongs to the latter class, and the association of his name with the fashion of the moment is used both when his speech is offered as the new style and when he proposes the cutting-down of Mankind's long gown. As to the name of Nowadays, it speaks for itself. As Peter points out, 'in these days' was a key expression in complaints of the contemporary world: 'one can trace it from Latin *hodie* through Middle English verse to the Morality Plays – in *Mankind* it achieves apotheosis as a character, Now-A-Days.'[46] There is much insistence on the names of the three when they appear. First, Nowadays says:

> Say not ageyn the new gyse nowadays!
> (107)

(where 'not' is presumably meant for 'nought'). Then Nought says:

> I herde yow call 'New Gyse, Nowadays, Nought,
> all thes thre togethere.
> (111)

Finally, they actually give their names in response to Mercy's question. This passage comes after a gap in the manuscript; so it is not clear whether

Mercy *did* call, or not. But it would make good sense if Mercy had, in the missing part of the text, been condemning the evils of the age in the manner characteristic of preachers in the moral plays. If Mercy had been responding to Mischief's challenge with some fulminations against the meaninglessness and folly of the modern world with all its mindless seeking after new excitements and fashions, then the appearance of the three would come as an ironic embodiment of the words he had been using.

Whether or not this is so, the three present an essentially satirical interpretation of the World. In most plays in which the World is characterised, it is represented in terms of riches and power. The main idea used in the moral plays in that the World exploits man's desires for the vanities of temporal position and luxury; the World's lures are command, money and goods; its great sin is Covetousness and its boasts are of possession.

> For I am rychest in myne araye.
> I have knyghtes and toures,
> I have ladyes bryghtest in bourys.
> (*Mundus et Infans*, 232–4)

It is striking, therefore, that in *Mankind* the World is represented by three scruffy, scrounging villains, who convey from the start an idea of the World which is sordid and vain. The best they can offer is lack of boredom, but this is based on crude horseplay and vapid mockery, and a mindless pleasure of comfort, sleep, taverns and women, which is offered in such shabby form that there is little temptation about it; also there are many contrary associations, of sterile mockery of virtue and the life of the mind, of physical violence, of coarseness and crudity, deceit and eventually crime. Even the bright promise of novelty and up-to-date excitement is soon dimmed by the evidence of their meaningless bustle. The literary associations they bring to mind are mainly of the satirical complaint tradition; they are a bridge between such demons as appear in *Jacob's Well* to distract man from pious thoughts and later pictures of the world, such as occur in Barclay's *The Ship of Fools*, as a place dominated by greed, malice and folly. Their mockery of learning, morality, Latin, Law-courts, friars, work and so on, accumulate motifs which combine the gleeful hatred of good usual to demons with the righteous condemnation of abuses of church and law usual to scornful preachers. This gives them that slightly mixed quality which can create some sympathy in the audience at moments. The shadows of the World's usual concern with wealth occur in the frequent references to money and theft and worldly possession, but the picture of the world's pomps is a debased one. No explicit role is given to their commander, Mischief; he is associated both with folly and with despair and becomes master of ceremonies in some moments, increasing the sense that vice is a kind of game.

The picture of the World in *Mankind*, is reinforced by the treatment of the Flesh and the Devil. Though there is, eventually, a reference to a mistress and a tavern, the Flesh is sadly unalluring in the play, and there is none of the sense of the pleasure of satisfying fleshly appetite for food and drink. This is a play about Sloth, and so it is understandable that the other sins of the Flesh, Lechery and Gluttony, are not prominent, but even Sloth does not afford Mankind much delight. The sense of the Flesh is present in the play as an aspect of Mankind himself: this is unusual, psychologically convincing and effective in moral terms. But it also has a satirical effect, in that Mankind's greatest weakness is treated as comically trivial. There is no lure in the Flesh, only filth and weakness, represented in the frequent references to bodily needs, in the joke that Mankind's resolve is not even strong enough to resist the need to void his bowels, in the association of the Vices with babyish language and with lavatorial humour.

The third member of the trio has more panache, but is not a very impressive Devil; he is penniless, introduced to the audience more or less as a peep-show, and has a relationship to the Vices rather like that of Fagin and his boys. His great act of corrupting Mankind is achieved by comic business with a plank, diarrhoea and lies. One can hardly feel that the Prince of Darkness is given much of a chance to create any real sense of a battle between good and evil.

What then does this amount to? One could argue that the playwright does not take his subject seriously and merely exploits the situations for scurrilous fun and farce; some have thought so. But I see it as more defensible. The dramatist has imagined the vanity of World, Flesh and Devil as largely negative. Mankind's sins are of omission; he is lured by the ease of not doing, rather than the temporary pleasure of doing. In order to create a sense of the pulling to and fro of Mankind, the figure of Mercy is made an object of derision within the world of the play, and the powers of evil are given sympathetic moments, through colloquial vigour, an impression of reality, comic quips and rapid movement. But as the play proceeds the moral view of the world becomes clearer, as vice turns into evil and mockery into crime. The satirical climax is the court-scene, where the element of parody gives spice to Mankind's swearing of allegiance to evil; the acts which he promises to perform are those which elsewhere are castigated as 'the way of the world nowadays'. Like Chaucer, the dramatist knows that he does not have to tell us so. He can leave irony to do its work.

The Towneley *Mactacio Abel* is another play which works by irony and which leaves an impression which is disturbing and which has appeared equivocal to some. Here too the voice of virtue is presented in a style which appears lifeless in comparison to that of vice. Abel's speeches are those of a puppet, expressing appropriate sentiments about tithes and duty to God. Cain's speeches are vigorous and colloquial, but also blasphemous and obscene. In itself the contrast of speech may be explained as a use for Cain of the style of the demons with whom he is by tradition associated, but the combination of a surly, grudging and abusive Cain with an impudent servant-boy and some farcical stage action makes it more complex. The Wakefield Master, like the author of *Mankind*, has set himself to represent the nature of evil, and the figure of Cain is one of the most powerful expressions of the ugliness of sin in medieval drama. To contain this portrait within the moral framework of the Cycle he could also have built up the role of Abel (or possibly of God) and created a strong dialogue between two equal opponents. He has taken instead what, in some ways, is the easier course, and has chosen to contain Cain by satirical distance. The satire works in several ways. The most important is achieved through the figure of the servant, Garcio, whose function it is to counter-act evil's pride in itself by trivialising mockery. Despite Cain's vehemence, it is the futility of evil which he eventually exemplifies. The element of protest in this futility has the power to draw in some of the audience's sympathy, through a second satirical strand, the ironic parallels between Biblical characters and the contemporary audience: Cain's protests against the sacrifice of his sheaves to God express fifteenth-century anti-clerical feeling; some of the colloquial language is designed to give realism to Cain as a farmer, and even after the murder he uses homely references designed to encourage a feeling of local knowledge:

> And hardely when I am dede,
> Bery me in Goody Bower at the Quarell Hede,
> For may I pas this place in quarte,
> Bi all men set I not a fart.
>
> (366–9)

This aids the impression that evil is sordid and mean, perhaps, but familiar and near-at hand.

The climax of this mixture of evil and comedy is the double act of Cain and Garcio at the end, where Cain makes a proclamation of pardon for the two of them and Garcio undercuts his rhetoric in alternate lines. The boy's interruptions are mainly irrelevant and deflating, but that is an off-hand preparation for the one line that completes the sense (with just what Cain wants unsaid):

Caym The kyng will that they be safe.

Garcio Yey, a draght of drynke fayne wolde I hayfe.

Caym At there awne will let tham wafe.

Garcio My stomak is redy to recayfe.

Caym Loke no man say to thaym, or non other–

Garcio This same is he that slo his brother.

> (428–33)

The effect of the play is, in some sense, to hold vice up to scorn, though sarcasm and deflation are directed more against Cain's blasphemy and miserliness than against murder. There is no process of repentance, as there is in the allegorical plays, and if one regards the episode in the context of the sequence of the Old Testament material in the cycle, the pageant is incomplete. But the Wakefield Master's treatment is, as Rosemary Woolf puts it, 'self-consciously artful'.[47] It works as a sardonic moral play in its own right and its ending is appropriate. Cain provides his own comment in a mood we meet again in another comic drama about damnation, *Don Giovanni*:

> Now fayre well, fellows all, for I must nedis weynd,
> And to the dwill be thrall, warld withoutten end.
> Ordand there is my stall, with Sathanas the feynd.   (462–7)

The main current of satire at the end of the fifteenth and the beginning of the sixteenth century seems to have been towards commentary on specific social and political events, particular people, and items of 'local' interest. Skelton is the most important satirist in the period and his attacks on Wolsey the outstanding instances of 'localised' satire. Medwall's *Nature* and two plays of the early sixteenth century, *Youth* and *Hick Scorner*, show how such satire had developed (with *Mankind* as a forerunner) into a particular type of play.

Ian Lancashire has shown that the two shorter plays were, like *Nature*, intended for indoor 'banquet' performance, that both were probably composed by a 'house' playwright for a particular household and that both are packed with local and contemporary references.[48] *Youth* was written 1513–14, perhaps in the Beverley area for the Percy household. *Hick Scorner* could have been written for Charles Brandon, created Duke of Suffolk in 1514, and, if Lancashire is correct, could be seen as an attack on Richard de la Pole, Brandon's predecessor. Drawing on several sources, including *Nature* and *Everyman*, the author of *Youth* concentrates, in a compact 800-line interlude, on the follies of a young rake, who rejects the advice of Charity and takes as companions Riot (habitué of taverns, fresh from Newgate and Tyburn), Pride and Lechery; Youth attacks and fetters Charity, who is rescued by Humility, the agent of Youth's spiritual recovery. The moral allegory is, at some points, perfunctory, and the playwright's real interest is social and political; he is probably using the framework of the moral play to comment on the extravagance, bodily vanity and wilfulness of the young Henry VIII. *Hick Scorner*, which uses material from *Youth*, is dramatically the more interesting of the two, but is essentially the same type of play. Like *Mankind* it creates two different moral worlds. First the three virtuous characters, Pity, Contemplation and Perseverance complain of the abuses of the age, the cruelty of the rich, widows forced into second marriage, lack of fear of death, the failure of the clergy. They are succeeded by three sinful figures,

Freewill, Imagination and Hick Scorner, who create the atmosphere of
taverns, stews and the London docks. They fetter Pity, who moralises:

> Lo, lordes, they may curs the tyme they were borne,
> For the wedes that over-groweth the corne.[49]
>
> (545–6)

and complains 'Worse was hyt never!', as he begins the familiar motif of
the reversals of virtue:

> Alas! now is lechery called love, in dede,
> And murdure named manhode in every
>   nede;
> Extorsyon is called lawe, so God me spede!
> Worse was hyt never!
>
> (557–60)

The liveliest scene in the play is the conversion of Freewill. This begins
with his boasts of cheating and theft in London, and proceeds via a 'Hey,
trolly, lolly!', to scorn for Pity, Contemplation and Perseverance:

> What! whome have we here?
> A priest, a doctoure, or else a frere?
> What, mayster doctour Dotypoll!

He is seized by the virtues, who bid him repent. He protests:

> What, ye dawes, wolde ye rede me
> For to lese my pleasure in youth and jolyte,
> To busse and kysse my swete trully mully,
> As Jane, Cate, Besse and Sybble to?
>
> (734–7)

In a number of lengthy speeches, which have the effect of a poetic
dramatic monologue more than a scene in a play, Freewill reveals his
trivial, vain, sinful life of petty enjoyment, trickery and crime. He is
gradually worn down from cockiness to penitence. The process is then
repeated, more briefly and less interestingly, with Imagination. Hick
Scorner does not re-appear.

The treatment of the conflict between virtue and vice here is prominent-
ly satirical. There is a good deal of comic realism in the references to the
low-life of London and of empty-headed young men who scorn religion.
The three figures of vice are brothers of New Guise, Nowadays and
Nought, but they have also absorbed the figure of Mankind. This brings
the play closer than the earlier fifteenth-century ones to the *Psychomachia*
idea of a battle between good and evil impulses in the mind, but the odd
construction of the work and the combination of personifications of

mental faculties with the type-figure Hick Scorner leaves the work unfocused; it suggests a writer whose interest was in realistic satire but who didn't quite know what to do with it. Again Lancashire suggests that it is in contemporary reference that the focus is to be found; if Hick Scorner is representative of Richard de la Pole, 'the land's greatest gangster, . . . the current Yorkist pretender to the throne',[50] then the play may be seen as a series of sketches of Tudor rogues, whose point is a satirical reflection of the times. Neither of these is as carefully worked-out a play as *Mankind*, but both show the satirical, social, contemporary tendency in medieval plays about sinful conduct. From the exhortation to repentance and the illustration of sin, it is a short step to using drama as a means of exposing specific vice and folly. Many plays include satirical elements, but the ones I have described go further and shape their material into a view of society or the World or earthly life which is ironic, jaundiced and bitter. Comedy, word-play, complaint, scorn and scurrility accumulate into a contemptuous attitude to the contemporary world.

4. *Comedy*

It seems more appropriate to me, and certainly it is more interesting, to discuss *Mankind* as an example of medieval comedy than as an example of the 'morality play'. The morality play aspects of the work represent a kind of lowest common denominator shared with the other Macro plays and the rest, whereas the comedy aspects represent the playwright's impulse towards experiment and the development of the dramatic possibilities of the theme of sloth. The qualities which used to make critics feel that this was the least serious of the moral dramas are those which show that the writer was alive to dramatic needs and not only to didactic ones. They are not the mark of a cynical exploitation of low comedy but an attempt to translate moral ideas into action and dialogue instead of simply asserting them. The play is an exemplary comedy in which the protagonist is misled and learns from his experience. The didactic aspect is strong but is made to develop from character and situation. Mankind's experience is express- ed in comedy, in his humiliation when he is tricked, abused and changed in nature and appearance, and in the suffering which makes the words of Mercy at the end necessary rather than tacked on.

As part of the creation of a comic exemplum, the dramatist makes use of several types of comic effect. There are scenes which depend on a contrast of manners, particularly the contrast between styles of speech. Woven through the scenes in which the Vices are involved are several themes of medieval satire and the cumulative effect is to create a view of the world which is contemptuous. Worldly activity is characterised as scruffy and grasping: the Vices engage in a mindless search for profit and empty pleasure. They are the spokesmen for the literal, physical world and the senses, as opposed to the world of the spirit, which is expressed through metaphor, symbol and a rich luxuriance of verbal resource. The consistent treatment of worldly activity, and the related deflation of the flesh and the Devil, make this one of the few medieval satirical comedies, not just a religious play with some satirical speeches.

In other plays of the period we can find some of the same elements and ideas of comedy. Though one does not know exactly what the original Paternoster Plays were, it seems plausible to suggest that exemplary plays illustrating one area of evil could have developed from the earlier idea of plays which presented each petition of the Lord's Prayer as a specific against a particular sin. Some plays do function in this way; they concentrate on one sin and use a story, presented in dialogue, to enact a moral lesson, through the course of and the remedy for sin. Such exemplary comedies are not necessarily very *funny*. They are comedies because they have a particular form and kind of plot, because they use comic intrigue, because the Devil exploits, with malicious glee, human weakness and provides the ironic pleasure of seeing his plotting eventually fail, and so on. They also tend to deal with behaviour in quite a lively and realistic way, which is often racy and pungent, if not especially humorous. Even satire is not often of the kind that raises a laugh; it can be merely condemnatory, or scornful, or bitter. At its best it shows the way of the world through caricature and other forms of exaggeration and fantasy. At its most frequent, it is given life by the vigorous style of the Devil, whose voice is used to expose the follies of mankind.

However, one does find humour and funniness in medieval plays. Drama is funniest in basic ways – in the love of farce and knock-about, in irreverence and surprise, in stock figures, such as comic servants, whom we are always prepared to find laughable, even in sheer bustle. In *Mankind* the physical aspect of comedy is important and in itself it distinguishes the play from the two others in the Macro manuscript. The play uses a lot of minor props (spade, grain, paper with writing, beads, scourge, plank, weapons and chains, dish and platter, rope, purses, flute, pen and paper, etc.) and this is a mark of a realistic, comic text. There is a fair amount of stage activity – tripping-up, the plank in the ground, the mock beheading, the botched suicide, and the general air of noise and frantic haste in the scenes with the Vices. The use of the theatre as well as the acting area and some tricks of sophisticated illusion add to the sense of comic experience: voices off occur several times; characters speak from the audience; Titivillus is meant to be invisible and this presumably should add a lot of humour, not expressed in the words, to the digging scene. All of these devices are used relevantly and discriminatingly in relation to the serious subject-matter of the play.

The degree to which various types of comedy are used with discrimination in *Mankind* may be measured by comparison with the uses of humour in some contemporary plays. A particularly revealing comparison is with another of the 'miscellaneous' plays of the period, the Croxton *Play of the Sacrament*.[51] This tells the story of the desecration of the Host by Jews, who are converted to Christianity at the end of the play. The legend had a continental origin. The version in the English play has five Jews, led by Jonathas, bribe a merchant in Aragon, called Aristorius, to steal the Consecrated Host from the church while his priest is asleep. The Jews then subject the 'cake' to stabbing, boiling in oil and roasting in an oven; at each stage the Host reacts, first with an effusion of blood and by sticking to Jonathas' hand (which his friends pull off in their frenzy), secondly by filling the cauldron with blood, and thirdly by splitting the oven and changing into 'an image', which must 'appere owt with woundys bledyng'. Jonathas and the other Jews are converted by this miracle, by the speech of Jesus, and by the traditional dramatic character Episcopus, who controls the last part of the play, hears the confession of merchant and priest, christens the Jews, and exhorts all with resolute and pious thoughts. This material is presented in a very odd way; it sounds in outline like a devout miracle-play, but in fact it is, for much of the time, farcical.

The points of comparison with *Mankind* are several. *The Play of the Sacrament* was written by another East Anglian playwright; apart from linguistic evidence, there is a reference to Babwell Priory, a Franciscan house a mile or two from Bury St Edmunds, on the road to Thetford in Norfolk, three miles from Croxton, which is mentioned in the banns.[52] It was probably written at about the same time as *Mankind*, a few years after 1461. Its manuscript paper shares a water-mark with that of *Mankind* (and part of the N-Town cycle). There is some aureate language in the play, as well as a combination of piety and farce which is similar, in some respects, to the combination in the Macro play. It seems possible, therefore, that the two plays are based on roughly similar ideas of theatre, audience and style.

The most startling scene is one that could perhaps be a later addition, but there it is as a central scene in the play, whenever and however it got there. It is a farcical routine between a comic Doctor and his servant Coll, who appear after Jonathas cannot leave go of the Host ('Her he renneth wood, with the Ost in hys hand', as the stage direction says) and has his hand torn off by his friends. Coll enters first and characterises his master as a great frequenter of ale-houses, with a good bedside manner with ladies, one of whom he is busy 'curing' at this moment. When the Doctor arrives, he gets Coll to make a proclamation, touting for custom. Coll obliges in the traditional cheeky servant manner:

> All maner of men that have any syknes,
> To Master Brent-berecly loke that yow redresse.
> What dysease or syknesse that ever ye have,
> He wyll never leve yow tyll ye be in your grave.
>
> (608–11)

After some comic dialogue, the two offer to cure Jonathas, but, evading Coll's efforts to get a urine sample, he shoos them out and they disappear from the play. This combination of satire on doctors and knockabout farce is obviously an example of gratuitous comedy, and we could dismiss it as merely a 'popular' interpolation of a comic doctor scene from the folk play tradition, were it not that there is a good deal of comedy elsewhere. The play begins in an almost completely secular style, with first the merchant Aristorius boasting of his merchandise (with luxuriant splendour conveyed through a catalogue of exotic place-names), and then Jonathas boasting of his possessions (with more verbal splendour from a catalogue of jewels and another of spices, with much alliteration and fine flourishes of foreign vocabulary). The plot to obtain the Host is developed by comic intrigue: Aristorius plies his Priest with potent wine – he, in the obliging way stage characters have to have, is immediately overcome with drowsiness and retires to bed, leaving the Merchant to rob the church in the small hours. The scenes in which the Jews torture the Host, potentially sinister and sacrilegious, are grotesque in a ludicrous way. The Jews are treated as cartoon figures crying:

> Have at yt! Have at yt wyth all my myght!

and when the Host bleeds:

> Ah! owt! owt! harrow! what devyll ys thys?

The scenes are full of exclamations, panic and pantomime. Only at the end, when Jesus appears, does the play settle into seriousness: at line 717 the mood switches totally and from then on the playwright conscientiously and laboriously pursues a homiletic course of solemn religious observance and exhortation to 'fyght agayn the fell serpent'.[53]

Compared to this mish-mash of didacticism and farce, *Mankind* is an intellectual and well constructed play. But even with such humour that occurs in *The Play of the Sacrament*, it is necessary to give a more important place than is at present the usual case to comedy in medieval drama. The Croxton play is crude, but the writer is trying to find a way of turning a chronicle into watchable stage life. He does not think of himself as writing a solemn liturgical ritual, it is clear, but a drama which presents an instructive example of the power of Christianity. For such an exemplary experience, comedy is the appropriate mode. He does not control the mode well, but the aim is apparent. When a dramatist controls the relationship between slapstick and exemplification better, as in *Mankind*, then it is no longer at all a matter of the 'addition' of comic effects to serious subject matter, but rather the perception within Scriptural and moral material of patterns of the development of understanding, for which comedy is the appropriate tone and the appropriate name.

The consciousness of comedy as a dramatic kind grows rapidly in the sixteenth-century interludes. One can see the direction it will take indicated in another late medieval 'medley'-play, Henry Medwall's *Fulgens and Lucrece*.[54] The length of this play is not the result of a comprehensive moral intention on Medwall's part, but is caused by his use of two levels of action: the comic by-play of servants acts as a contrast to and a comment on the situations of their masters. The serious centre of the play is a debate between the rival claims of the suitors of Lucrece who represent different social and political *mores*; the older aristocratic virtues are placed in antithesis with those of modern pragmatism in a 'disputacyon' about gentility. This seems to us both characteristically 'medieval' (in its echoes of Chaucer's Wife of Bath) and 'humanist' (in its dependence on a Latin treatise and the classical dispute in general). The play's significance to the history of English drama is that the treatment of the material is moral without being specifically religious and that the 'serious' secular comedy of manners and morals is accompanied by the parody and slapstick of the subplot of comic rivalry between the suitors' servants, called A and B, who act as Chorus, the audience's representatives, interrupters and mockers, and providers of the spirit of games, songs and pastimes. The accompaniment of the moral debate by a 'sub-plot' which supposedly begins outside the fictional world of the play and then crosses over into it hints at a greater sophistication in Medwall's sense of the relationship between actor and audience than tends to be found in earlier plays; it is of interest, in this respect, as a forerunner to *The Knight of the Burning Pestle* and other comic Elizabethan exploitations of the physical realities of the playhouse. Medwall thus may be said, at least to a limited extent, to recognise 'even if indirectly, a distinction between art and life, the actor and his audience, which now required a new, secular interpretation'.[55]

It is a laboured work, however; Medwall has little verbal skill and to see the play as the herald of any new dawn is to exaggerate its merits. But placing it beside *Mankind* and other examples of medieval and Renaissance comedy helps one to see how Elizabethan comedy grew from medieval origins. Partly it is a growth in liveliness and variety of stage action, in the dramatist's impulse to diffuse the plot into a series of scenes designed to create entertainment from the illustration of folly and vice. The moral thesis of the play may turn from being the main channel along which action flows into a theme with variations; so play may be accompanied by a kind of anti-play, and the moral conflict within man between virtue and vice may be envisaged as a relationship between two worlds. *Mankind* is already moving in that direction; Medwall, like Skelton, goes further along the same road by extending moral divisions into social ones.

Another sign of growth is the development from an interest in the choices within man into an interest in the choices between men. This involves the significant step from allegorical figures representing parts of human nature to 'individual' human beings representing a more complex mixture of moral elements. One of the most interesting activities for the student of early drama is to observe how theatrical means change and yet retain qualities of earlier instances. If one reads, say, *The Merchant of Venice* with these medieval comedies in mind, one can see how Bassanio is the descendant not only of Gaius Flaminius, the plebeian suitor in Medwall's play, but also (however ambiguous the result) of the virtuous phases of the Mankind figures, as opposed to the allegorical representatives of pride and worldliness, how Portia is the descendant not only of Lucrece, but also of personifications of virtue, such as Mercy in *Mankind*, and how Gratiano and Launcelot Gobbo grew not only from such figures as A and B, but also from the earlier disruptive vices, such as New Guise, Nowadays and Nought.

CHAPTER FOUR

Wisdom *and the Drama of Ideas*

1. *Wisdom*

The play now usually known as *Wisdom* and grouped with *The Castle of Perseverance* and *Mankind* under the label 'The Macro Plays' used to be identified as *Mind, Will and Understanding* and could be grouped with *The Conversion of St Paul, Mary Magdalene* and *The Killing of the Children* under the label 'the Digby Plays', except that the copy of the play which appears in MS Digby 133 is incomplete. In the modern edition, which adds a few lines to the Macro text from the Digby version, it consists of 1163 lines, written mainly in 8-line stanzas, most of which are either Monk's stanza or tail-rhyme. Its language is literary, without being exaggeratedly ornate or aureate, though there is a fair number of Latin lines. Any suggestion that it is a 'popular' play sorts ill with the literary tone. It is a religious play composed as a series of talking and moving pictures. Though there are no scene-divisions marked in either manuscript, the play falls into four distinct phases: twice the stage becomes completely empty (at line 324 and line 550), so that it is natural to see scene-divisions there, and the re-entry of Wisdom, after a long absence, at line 873 so obviously marks a crucial turning-point in the play that it seems appropriate to make a scene-division after line 872. I shall treat it, therefore, as Eccles does, as a play in four scenes.[1] The sense of scene is important in another sense, since the elaborate stage-directions and details of appearance are a striking feature of the text.

The first scene (1–324) begins with a tableau, which could be taken from a medieval manuscript or stained-glass window, of Christ in majesty, dressed in purple and ermine, adorned with a wig, eyebrows and beard of gold, and furnished with a bejewelled crown and golden orb and sceptre. He identifies himself as Wisdom, God the Son, 'now Gode, now man', the Spouse of the elect soul. Anima, the soul of man, then appears, as a maiden richly dressed in a fur-adorned white dress, made of cloth-of-gold, and a black mantle, and with an elaborate garland with gold tassels upon another gold wig. The religious material of the opening scene is thus presented through figures of majesty and splendour: it is clear that Anima is, if not Christ's equal, at least worthy to be his beloved. The other-worldly perfection of the heavenly kingdom and of the purity of the love between God and the soul are represented, as in the dream-poem *Pearl*, partly by the aesthetic appeal of the symbols of worldly wealth and luxury.

The pictorial quality of the scene is enhanced by the language of the two speakers, as they begin to express their love. Anima speaks of love in terms of goodness, beauty and brightness, and the imagery is taken up by Wisdom, whose brightness is the mirror of Divine goodness and power, and whose worthiness is everlasting and richer than all worldly possessions:

> The lengthe of the yerys in my ryght syde be,
> Ande in my left syde ryches, joy and prosperyte.   (36–7)

His love is also sweeter and more wholesome than, and takes away all delight in, worldly pleasures, so that:

> Wo tastyt therof the lest droppe sure,
> All lustys and lykyngys worldly xall lett;
> They xall seme to hym fylthe and ordure.   (50–2)

Anima's fervent, lyrical expression of love to her 'swet amyke' has its climax in the question:

> Wat may I yeve yow ageyn for this,
> O Creator, lover of yowr creature?   (73–4)

and receives the reply:

> Thy clene hert, thi meke obeysance,
> Yeve me that and I am contente.   (81–2)

The emphasis here is much more emotional and intense than is the case in the other allegorical plays of the period. There is no opening sermon, but a poetic expression of the love between Christ and the soul. The combination of the luxurious splendour of the figures' appearance and the intensity of the imagery in their speech provides *Wisdom* with an opening which makes a powerful impression on both eye and ear.

From line 86 the course of the dialogue becomes more clearly didactic, as Wisdom responds to Anima's request for enlightenment, but the nature of the religious instruction is distinctive, though belonging to an important medieval tradition of Christian teaching. As the expression of love between Christ and the soul reminds the reader of the emphasis on Christ as lover in the verse and prose of Rolle and in earlier works for devout women such as *The Wooing of Our Lord*, the Katherine Group and *Ancrene Wisse*, so the answer to Anima's question about God's incomprehensible divinity is couched in terms of the instruction of their disciples by other mystical writers, especially, in this case, Walter Hilton.[2] Stress is on instinct and feeling rather than intellect: knowledge comes from awe of God, submission to his will and the knowledge of self in the 'sowle sensyble' and the 'self passyble'. The idea of the 'sensible' soul, which is capable of emotion and of suffering ('passyble') is an ancient one, coming originally from Aristotle, and accepted by medieval philosophers as a basic distinction from the rational soul. What Wisdom teaches is that one must know God through one's own soul, since the soul is an image of God, and was, until Adam's fall, the fairest of things; from the death of Wisdom, who redeemed the Fall, come the sacraments, through which the blemished soul may recover its first beauty. The distinction between parts of the soul is made more specific as Wisdom teaches the relationship between sensuality ('fleschly felynge' together with the five senses – the 'outewarde wyttys' which need controlling) and reason (the image of God). These two aspects of the soul are symbolised by Anima's garb: the black cloak represents sensuality and the white dress reason:

> Thus a sowle ys bothe fowlle and fayre:
> Fowll as a best be felynge of synne,
> Fayer as a angell, of hevyn the ayer,
> By knowynge of Gode by hys reson wythin.   (157–60)

This phase of the scene is brought to an end in spectacle, music and quotation, as five white-clad maidens (representing the five senses) enter and sing 'I am black but comely, O ye daughters of Jerusalem' from the Song of Songs. The blackness is interpreted by Anima as 'this dyrke schadow I bere of humanyte', and Wisdom bids Anima keep clean the five senses:

> For the clene sowll ys Godys restynge place.   (176)

I have described the material of this first part of the scene in some detail, because I think that *Wisdom* is the only one of the early English allegorical plays which handles religious concepts in an intellectual (or even in an intelligent) way and which is capable of engaging the audience's interest in ideas. The key to the playwright's power of involving one in the nature of the inner life is his combination of literary imagery in the speeches with effective stage imagery. The idea of the dual nature of the soul is focused through costume and colour symbolism; the beauty of Christ's love is represented by splendour of appearance and the making of a rich tableau by grouping and the contrast between Wisdom's purple and gold and the white of the senses and Anima's black and white. The scene is mainly static and it is easy to see, from even part of a scene, why Eccles and others have tended to disparage the play with such comments as:

Wisdom is too intent on teaching moral virtue to have much concern with dramatic virtues. The author combines preaching with pageantry . . .[3]

But the comment is based on a narrow idea of what 'dramatic virtues' are. The virtues of *Wisdom* are akin to the virtues of masque, or even to those of the later forms of opera and ballet: *Wisdom* is the medieval play most easily envisaged as ballet, despite the loss of lyrical and explanatory passages which would result from the translation, because the essential elements of the play are expressed visibly. The opening dialogue presents the simple, powerful symbolism of black and white as the key to the relationship between God and the soul. Love's link with purity is established in one's mind, before a representative of bodily humanity appears. It is consistent with the quality of this religious approach (and its origin in mystical instruction and analysis of the inner conflict of the anchorite who must learn to approach God) that, when it does appear, humanity is represented in tripartite form, as a trio of the 'mights' of the soul, which are the reflection in man of the Trinity.

The three powers of the soul are Mind, Understanding and Will, and together they perform the function of Humanum Genus or Mankind or Everyman. The division of man into his constituent parts inevitably means that *Wisdom* is less easily grasped than the other plays mentioned. This play is not concerned with creating 'life-like' effects through its allegorical figures; if it has any quality of realism, it is simply the realism of a traditional psychology of the human faculties. Each of the three mights is given a speech of four stanzas, as soon as he appears, in which his function is defined. Mind explains that he is the true figure of God in the soul, and is the seat of man's awareness; he is thought, the cognitive faculty, and also memory. Through Mind man understands his sinfulness, instability and frailty, and his need for gratitude to God. The complexity of the concept is represented through academic word-play on the various senses of *mynde* in the last stanza of the four.

Will speaks second, because the contrast is clearer between Mind and Will than between Mind and Understanding, and we can thus see Mind and Will as the two outer extremes, with Understanding in the middle. The word *will* was the subject of puns long before Shakespeare made play with it (in Langland, for instance) and it runs through all four stanzas of Will's speech, as he distinguishes between the will and the deed, and stresses the need for will to be good will. Without God, man's will is corrupt:

> For of owrselff we have ryght nought
> But syne, wrechydnes, and foly.   (234–5)

Understanding is the intermediary between Mind and Will, the part that experiences (i.e. *connaître*, where Mind is *savoir*). His speech is the least explanatory of the three and makes little use of verbal wit; he speaks in praise of God and learning to know God through 'knowynge of me' and through experience of God's love:

> Thus wndyrstondynge of Gode compellys
> To cum to charyte.   (273–4)

Wisdom completes the exposition of the concepts upon which the play is built with a series of interpretations. Mind, Understanding and Will are each and all similitudes of God – Mind of the Father, Understanding of the Son, and Will, 'wyche turnyt into love brennynge', of the Holy Ghost. Mind is the means of Faith, Understanding of Hope and Will of Charity. Above these is man's free will, through which, if it is perverted, all may be destroyed. The three enemies are World, Flesh and Devil, against whom the three powers are warned:

> Wan suggestyon to the Mynde doth apere,
> Wndyrstondynge, delyght not ye therin;
> Consent not, Wyll, yll lessons to lere.   (301–3)

The scene is brought to an end by two rhetorical stanzas from Anima, expressing love, gratitude, praise and prayer in a ritualistic series of lines:

> Wan I was noght, thou made me gloryus . . .
> Wen I was ignorant, thou taut me truthe,
> Wen I go wyll, thou art my gyde . . .   (310 ff.)

Then all depart in a musical procession, led by the five senses, repeating their song, followed by Anima, then Wisdom, then the three mights of the soul, who also, we are now told, are dressed in white, bewigged and garlanded.

The scene thus continues to depend on pictures and symbols as at the start; the latter part adds to symbolism of costume and colour the allegorical explanations and symbolic associations of Mind, Understanding and Will. Symbolism is augmented by images used to vivify religious ideas: love is seen as a burning fire, wisdom as the mirror of God's perfection, evil and good acts as weeds and herbs. These images bring with them associations from their earlier use in the writings of the fourteenth-century mystics and in other instructional texts. Considerable sophistication of literary intention is apparent in the use of rhetoric and word-play, as well as in the careful presentation of ideas and themes and the clear intellectual distinctions.

The figures have virtually no dramatic life of an individual, active or realistic kind, of course. They are used as static figures for the purposes of demonstration: this is especially obvious when Wisdom explains the significance of Anima's costume. They speak to express and to explain their natures and attitudes; the only important movements are the entry and the dance-song of the senses and the processional exit, and these are quite separate from the words. The dramatic life of the scene is found elsewhere. It is, first, in the picturesque aspects, which grip the imagination by their splendour and the mind by their emblematic power: meaning is conveyed through costume, tableau and explicit symbolism. Secondly, the scene works through patterning. This is found in the symmetry of the figures and speeches and the sense that figures are constantly being presented as part of numerical groups, as if to form a series of interlocking mathematical designs.[4] Wisdom is part of the Trinity, is simultaneously God and man; the Soul has a dual nature of black and white, and has three powers; the sensible part of the soul in turn has its five senses. So the classifications multiply and interlock by means of the reminders that man and his various faculties are all images of God and aspects of the soul. The patterning in the figures is reflected in the composition of the scene, in the use of speeches of similar length for Mind, Understanding and Will, in patterned rhetoric, in the rhyme-patterning in the stanzas. The stylised effect of such features is supported by literary diction, academic word-play and Latin lines. The imagination also responds to the quality of formal debate and exposition which begins to characterise the play as a drama of ideas; one recognises that the poet's main aim is to express religious ideas in a tone which is heightened, sophisticated and literary.

The second scene (325–550) is the temptation and is, in some respects, in a more conventional mode, in that Lucifer dominates the scene and has the familiar function of turning Christian resolve into appetite for the World, the Flesh and the Devil. The terms in which these appetites are stirred are individual, however, and the scene shows careful composition and consistent literary intention.

We begin with Lucifer alone and the text's usual care about appearances is evident in the instruction that Lucifer must have a disguise already on beneath his 'devil's array'. A shift of metre into tail-rhyme stanzas and a shorter line gives the opening a brisk swing, as Lucifer identifies himself with a catch-phrase:

> Owt! harow! I rore,
> For envy I lore,
> My place to restore
>   God hath made a man.   (325–8)

As Devils and Vices usually do, he takes us into his confidence, explaining his envy and his history and his intention to tempt and beguile the powers of man's soul by exploiting their changeability, in order to defile and damn the soul:

> To the Mynde of the Soule I xall make suggestyun,
> And brynge hys Understondynge to dylectacyon,
> So that hys Wyll make confyrmacyon.   (365–7)

In order not to frighten man, Lucifer determines to 'change me into bryghtnes', which suggests both his former angelic glory and that he is aping the brightness which in Wisdom is the mirror of God's goodness; in the event a quick exit and return allows Lucifer to doff his Devil's garb and to reveal only the spurious worldly brightness of disguise as 'a goodly galont'. In this disguise he sets about Mind, Understanding and Will, who appear for once without a stage direction and have four pious lines apiece before the Devil goes to work. The temptation makes clear what the earlier announcement of intention had implied, that the three powers are mutually dependent and that the real temptation is of Mind. Once man's thought is convinced by intellectual argument, then Understanding will follow, by putting suggestion into the practice of experience, and Will will consent and satisfy sensual desire. Thus the first temptation, of Mind, is the most ingenious and the most dramatically interesting, and the one where some resistance to the Devil's persuasions is shown. There is no attempt at psychological realism and we are a long way from Iago and Othello, but, whereas Understanding and Will immediately respond to Lucifer's lures, Mind is given five rejecting speeches, and one half-way speech ('Truly, me seme ye have reson.') before yielding. Lucifer has to pursue the attack through a succession of speeches; his argument is thereby emphasised.

Since it is clear that the dramatist regards the perverting of Mind as the significant event, it is interesting that the terms in which Lucifer persuades Mind to change are those of an attack upon the contemplative life. What Lucifer presents is a reasoned argument for engagement in the common matters of life: a man with the practical responsibilities of family and affairs would be neglecting duty if he lived a life of ease and prayer. Jesus, we are reminded, was concerned with teaching and example rather than meditation; the exaggerated discipline of the enclosed life of prayer and contemplation is a way of folly leading to despair and madness:

> They must fast, wake, and pray ever new,
> Wse hard lywynge and goynge wyth dyscyplyne dew,
> Kepe sylence, wepe, and surphettys eschewe,
> And yff thay fayll of thys, they offende Gode hyghly.
> Wan they have wastyde by feyntnes,
> Than febyll ther wyttys and fallyn to fondnes,
> Sum into dyspeyer and sum into madnes.   (433–9)

In one way this argument is designed for Mind, as opposed to Understanding, since it is the mind that creates and lives in ivory towers. With a slightly different emphasis, we can interpret the temptation as directed against 'a fugitive and cloistered virtue', and as built on the beguiling idea that true virtue should be able to withstand the test of the market-place. But it is also possible that there is a literal appropriateness in the argument, and that the play was originally designed for a monastic or at least a clerical audience. Though Lucifer's speeches are not lengthy, they are cogent, forceful and interesting. This is true also of the speeches to Understanding and Will, though here there is an immediate response. Understanding is urged to let the five senses take pleasure in fine clothing, worldly power, riches and all of the conventional 'lust and

85

lykynge'. The advice is 'Se and beholde the world abowte!' (464). Similarly Will is urged to leave study and 'lede a comun lyff' with the usual pleasures:

> What synne ys in met, in ale, in wyn?
> Wat synne ys in ryches, in clothynge fyne?
> All thyng Gode ordenyde to man to inclyne.
> Leve yowr nyse chastyte and take a wyff.   (473–6)

The easy consent and hopeful delusion of the powers of the soul is summed up by Will:

> Man may be in the worlde and be ryght gode.   (486)

We know better, and watch with the usual sense of irony the beginnings of folly, as Lucifer bids them:

> A, ser, all mery than! awey care!   (500)

and sends them to change their sober long clothes ('that syde aray') into something jolly. Understanding responds with lively silliness:

> We woll be fresche, hanip la plu joly!
> Farewell penance!   (511–2)

Lucifer is left alone as the three go off stage to change, and he brings the scene to a close with four stanzas expressing his satisfaction, his intention of steering the mind of man into his own sin, that of pride, and his desire to make the soul 'Ewyn lyke to a fende of hell'. With a boast and a devilish theatrical flourish (snatching a naughty boy from the audience), he departs.

The scene is constructed to emphasise Lucifer. This is the only scene in which he appears, and he is its star. He begins and ends it, explains his intentions at the start and comments on his success at the end. The central section is an ironic demonstration of his power for which we have been prepared. If the scene is less picturesque and less full of heightened symbolic significance than the first, it nevertheless has its visual appeal in Lucifer's dual appearance and his final trick, and it contrasts well with the earlier scene through its emphasis on evil, its greater vigour of expression and the usual demonic touches of comedy and glee. The movement of the verse is racier, because of the tail-rhyme stanzas, and the expression clear and unfussy, with some lively phrasing and neat antithesis and patterning. The playwright is using conventional mechanisms, but handles them firmly within the formal, patterned structure of his dramatic mode, and gives to the temptation an individual cast in his intelligent use of the debate between the active and the contemplative life.

The third of the four scenes is the demonstration of the corruption of the soul's powers. One by one, Mind, Understanding and Will enter transformed into fashionable gallants: there is no stage direction here, but each boasts of his fresh, jolly array. Mind bids farewell to perfection, Understanding to conscience and Will to chastity. They exult in skipping mirth. Mind has become aloof and disdainful, proud of noble birth and worldly position. Understanding's joy is to hoard wealth and become a social climber by its means. Will's pleasure is in love, dalliance and disguise. After a song they egg each other on to describe their conditions. Mind reckons himself honoured by the service of mighty lords, by maintenance and influence; Understanding's successes are in bribery, perjury and simony, Will's in lust and uncleanness.

One might expect this part of the play to be most lively and inventive, since it is in illustration of sin that medieval playwrights are in general most pungent. The author of *Wisdom* is not, however, interested in devising vivid and realistic instances of vice (such as one finds in *Mankind*). There is no stage action in the early part of the scene. There are many familiar motifs of fifteenth-century social comment, but the satirical specification of worldly sin is presented formally, with the speeches in a symmetrical pattern. Mind, Understanding and Will open with a stanza each; then they have a second stanza, in the same order, then a half-stanza, then single or double lines, and so on, always in the same order. The dialogue is arranged in a dance-like sequence, or that of a musical canon. The figures do not enact vice, but offer a patterned display of attitudes. The cumulative effect is to picture the abuses of the age – social inequality, vanity of the nobility, the aristocracy's maintenance of private armies of retainers, corruption of law, indulgence in lechery – which together compose a tripartite complaint on the theme of 'The Way of the World Nowadays'. The three identify themselves as tenor, mean and treble for their song of mirth at line 620, and the musical relationship is one which could be metaphorically extended to the speeches; they are all singing the same song with merely a difference of voice. The dramatic power is in the stylised tableau and not in any mimetic depiction of human behaviour. By far the most effective aspect of the scene comes as the climax to these speeches in a set of allegorical dances, or dumb shows with music. It is here that the corruption of each is manifested (rather than just stated) on stage.[5]

The first of the three companies of dancers consists of six red-bearded figures, dressed like Mind, with lions rampant on their crests, each carrying a staff; they are accompanied by trumpets. The six are identified as Indignation and Sturdiness, Malice and Hastiness, Wretch and Discord; Mind himself has become the seventh in the gang, in the guise of Maintenance, and leads them in 'the Devil's dance'. The trumpets bring reminders both of battle and of Judgment, both of which are suited to 'thes meny of meyntement'. The company comprehends three sins, Pride, Envy and Wrath (the sins usually associated with the Devil). This masque of vice employs costume, heraldic symbolism, a symbolic staff, allegorical identification as well as the sinister ceremony of the dance itself. It conveys far more effectively than the preceding dialogue the nature of the Devil's influence on man. The associations are with violence and tyranny; even the musical instrument is condemning and vengeful.

The same means are used in the masque of the corruption of Understanding which follows. His own role is Perjury; his six attendants appear as hooded jurors, with two faces within their hoods to indicate the duplicity of law, and are identified as Wrong and Sleight, Doubleness, Falsehood, Raveyn (Robbery) and Deceit. Their father is Covetousness; their instrument the bagpipe (presumably because of the pun on bag, the receptacle for the bribe to go in) and their dance is presented as an endless progress of falsity and injustice by the 'quest of Holborn' (the Middlesex sheriff's jury), which, since the phrase is used twice, presumably had a name for corruption, and which can satirically represent the values of the world.

The third masque, of Will, does not make its identifications so explicitly, but the dramatist assumes that the pattern is clear enough for us to understand that Will is identified as Lechery and that the three sins which the company comprehends are those of the flesh: Sloth, Gluttony and Lechery. The six figures are unexpectedly described as women, who are in the same costume (or at least in the same colour, to be 'in sut') and divided into pairs, each composed of a gallant and a matron; the gallants are Recklessness, Idleness and Surfeit, the matrons Spousebreach, Mistress and Fornication. They are masked and accompanied by a horn-pipe (another pun intended obviously).

These three symbolic dances are, in stage terms, the most striking representations of vice in the early drama. The tradition from which they stem is that of court pageants and entertainments, which, like the 'subtleties' of court banquets, were often allegorical.[6] More particularly they may be seen as 'mummings' or 'disguisings', which could be civic pageants or tableaux, sometimes with speeches (as in the Mummings of Lydgate).[7] In *Wisdom* the dances need the preceding speeches to explain their significance, but the nature of the sins into which Mind, Understanding and Will have fallen receives its most vivid embodiment without words. The trio of seven figures transfer the number of the deadly sins to the sub-classes within sin, so that there is, as there was in the first scene, a sense of the interlocking of numerical classifications.

The scene is dominated by these allegorical pageants, but the break-up of the dance in quarrelsome chaos brings another aspect of vice to our attention: conflict and disorder in the soul. The planning by the three powers of their future careers of sin makes a brief gesture towards the satirical, contemporary realism that one finds in other plays: if Will hopes to find his satisfaction in the City stews, Understanding's place is in the law-courts of Westminster Hall, while Mind hopes to act the entrepreneur in the porch of St Paul's. Their idle vying chatter and their indulgence in vain thoughts of ease and wealth are less symmetrically arranged than the speeches before the dances, but the over-all effect of a diagram of attitudes, rather than an active embodying, is the same. One has only to compare the colloquialism, scurrility, slapstick and vicious-ness of *Mankind* to see how decorous and formal is the treatment of 'Life-in-Sin' in *Wisdom*. Idleness in corruption is identified, through boasting and folly, but the imagination is touched more by the dumb-show, despite the place-names and the flavour of city-life. True, the horizons are shown to be wider than those of East Anglia and Cambridge in *Mankind* but the dramatist's heart is not in it and the London world merely contributes a touch of particularity to a notional treatment of sin.

The entry of Wisdom after long absence instigates the last movement of the play, repentance and the cleansing of the soul. As soon as Wisdom warns Mind to turn, since death is certain, Mind rejects the life of sin. (This is of course one of the signs of the inevitability of allegory: wisdom has come to mind and this in itself *is* the intellectual recognition of wrong.) What is intellectually conceived cannot immediately be turned into effect, and there is here a distinction among the three powers: Understanding and Will are reluctant to accept Wisdom's message and need to be presented with the visual proof of their sin. This is provided by the entry of Anima, who appears 'fowlere than a fende', her 'horrible mantle' concealing seven (the MS says VI, but the Deadly Sins must be intended) small boys in the likeness of devils, who appear to demonstrate to the three powers just how they have defiled the Soul and how many sins there are within. Before the demons can be put to flight, the three must respond to Wisdom's warning and pleading:

> Why yewyst thou myn enmy that I have wrought?
> Why werkest thou hys consell? by myn settys lyght?
> Why hatest thou vertu? why lovyst that ys nought?
>
> (922–4)

In response the three express, in a stanza each, their recognition of sin.

Anima, who pleads to be made clean, is taught the cleansing power of the tears of contrition. She weeps; the demons retreat. She prays for mercy and submits to Mother Church; the demons depart. Singing in lament, 'wyth drawte notys as yt ys songyn in the passion wyke', Anima goes out and all but Wisdom follow. This section is the most effectively dramatised part of the final scene, because of its combination of symbolic stage movements, the concentration of precise religious feelings in a few speeches and actions, and the liturgical touches in the language and the music.

Left alone, Wisdom preaches (997–1064). The material is taken from a text on nine ways of pleasing God called *Novem Virtutes*, which was once attributed to Richard Rolle.[8] The speech is patterned: it consists of nine stanzas, with one given to each virtue. It is a completely static address to the audience. In a sense, it is a dramatic weakness to give so much space at the climax of the play to a homily where we become the recipients of the moral warning already heeded by our stage representatives. But it is far more in place in this stylised tableau than in more realistic types of moral drama and its emphasis on humility and the feelings of the individual heart takes us back to the affective piety and mystical teaching from which the play began. The speech is a lyric, beginning in simplicity with the idea that it is easy to please God: one has only to 'Gyff a peny . . . To the pore' and to weep one tear. Such spontaneous acts of feeling are the basis of charity and more pleasing to God than great deeds. The language becomes more elevated as the speech develops and the magnitude of the virtues grows, into the final act: 'Love me soverenly'. Thus the speech is both a sermon from Wisdom, in a priestly role, and a plea from Christ to man, asking for love. Because of this emotional strain, the speech asks for the audience's involvement, not just an acceptance of a moral lesson.

The play ends with a return to the processional splendour of the state of perfection from which man's soul began. Anima enters, preceded by the five senses, accompanied by Mind and Understanding on either side and followed by Will; all are dressed, crowned and garlanded as at first, and all sing a penitential psalm. Anima prays for compassion and confesses both the inward and the outward bodily offences against Christ: in reply Wisdom speaks (in his role of Son of God) of the way his senses make atonement for the wrongs of Anima and of his sufferings on the Cross:

> Myn hede bowhede down to kys the here;
> My body full of holys, as a dovehows.
> In thys ye be reformyde, soule, my plesere,
> Ande now ye be the very temple of Jhesus.   (1105–8)

Echoes of Rolle's *Meditations on the Passion* and of Passion Lyrics enrich the poetic effect of the speech.

Mind, Understanding and Will each speak a stanza to Anima, consisting of two opening lines in which the Soul is bidden to use her powers, then a Latin quotation from the Epistles of Paul, and ending with the Soul's renewal, respectively in 'gostly felynge', in reason and in 'Godys knowynge'. More quotations from the Vulgate are woven into the two stanzas with which Anima brings the play to a close, in praise of Wisdom, prayer and submission to God. In this latter section the playwright follows Hilton's teaching in *The Scale of Perfection*, as he had in the establishment of the nature of the soul in the first scene. So the play ends in Hilton's modest, sober stress on man's submission to God, buttressed in substance by the familiarity of Scripture, and elevated in tone by the resonance of the Latin tongue in which it was known.

The last part of the play again seems to make its strongest dramatic effects through visual symbolism, music and tableau. The pageant-like quality is dominant: there is no struggle, but a stylised demonstration of recognition of sin, repentance and reform. As before, the speeches are often symmetrically arranged and they are written to be effective as poetry and as oratory rather than as dialogue. The role of Wisdom is animated by rhetorical intensity, lyrical fervour and emphasis on suffering and feeling, so that the effect is not simply homiletic. The mystical stress on inward feeling, the response of the heart and mind to God's suffering and the sense of union between God and the awakened soul inform Wisdom's addresses both to Anima and to the audience. Finally, the poet seeks to convey a sacramental quality in the concluding stanzas through Latin (rather than aureate English) and his choice is apt. The result is that the play communicates religious faith and not simply a moral lesson about human conduct.

Wisdom is a play which attempts to convey Christian Charity and the idea of the soul's perfection through the symbolism of costume, dumbshow, dance and song in combination with religious material drawn from mystical teaching and emotional lyrics. It is a poetic drama and a set of patterns and pictures. As with the individual parts, so with the whole play: the construction is symmetrical. In the final scene the repeated procession, the return to Wisdom and Anima and to the theme of the love between God and the Soul reinforce the impression of the drama as a patterned dance of figures and themes. The central scenes of the play are simply an expansion of the ideas in Wisdom's initial teaching, as if the Soul has to re-live the loss of first perfection brought by Adam's sin: so the scenes grow, like flash-backs or a re-living of experience in dream. Of the medieval moral plays, this is the most suggestive and evocative of the sense that experience is a constant repetition of an existing pattern of being.

If we attempt to place *Wisdom* as a dramatic type, we have to identify it as an elaborate, sophisticated, literary play. At a later time it would be identifiable as a play for a children's company of actors or for the audience of the Inns of Court.[9] At this period, drama for a rich household, or for a University or Lawyers' Hall, or for a monastery school seem possibilities. It has none of the qualities of the popular play for a company of touring players. It is poetic, elaborate in expression and in design, and expensive in its requirements. The moral turning-point of the play is a brief review of criticisms of the contemplative life. This brings into the work some background of debate about works and prayer, about retirement from the world as opposed to the busy life of common activity; this takes one back to Rolle, Langland and Wycliffe and the concerns of fourteenth-century religious thinking, and beyond them to the Latin tradition of argument and writing about the nature of the religious life. Together with the treatment of human nature, this interest in the 'way' of life as a central aspect of virtue and vice on earth suggests an approach to the moral play which has a strong sense of literary tradition, and possibly also some sense of academic tradition.[10] The university debate is a possible influence, as well as devotional teaching about the relationship among the inner faculties and a concept of drama in terms of tableau, with music and dance. It is the only one of the early moral plays which uses allegory consistently and intelligently, and which avoids the acceptable but muddled idea of having an allegorical representative of man on stage at the same time as personifications of aspects of his nature. It is also the only play built around a vivid central image, that of the soul corrupted and made foul and ugly by the sins of the body. The appearance of the grotesque figure of Anima at the end of the play is quite as powerful a moment to the imagination as the effect of the portrait in *The Picture of Dorian Gray* and rather more universal in its application.

Wisdom is an under-rated play both in terms of its effectiveness as drama and also as a significant link in the chain of literary history. Through it one can connect the elaborate costuming and symbolism of masques, the theoretical element in medieval religious drama, which shows the seeds from which later 'humanist' debate-plays grew, and some survival of the ritualistic elements from earlier liturgical plays.

2.   *Closet-drama and Debate*

Another link in the historical chain of which I spoke above is 'the earliest academic drama extant in England', which forms an interesting comparison with *Wisdom*; unfortunately it is not in English, but in the medieval academic tongue, Latin.[11] This is *Liber Apologeticus de Omni Statu Humanae Naturae* (A Defence of Human Nature in Every State) written by Thomas Chaundler, who was Chancellor of the University of Oxford 1457–61 and 1472–9, Vice-Chancellor in the years between, holder of many livings and preferments, and a good academic administrator who looked after the finances and public position of New College well and who steered the University through some difficult times. His interest in writing in dramatic form was an interest in academic debate rather than in the stage; he also had some early 'humanist' interest in knowledge of Greek, at second-hand.[12] He was a graduate both in divinity and civil law, and while the latter is more prominent in his Latin poetic debate between Bath and Wells (his place of birth), *Libellus de laudibus duarum civitatum*, in which he shows an indirect knowledge of Plato's *Republic*, the two strains meet in the Latin prose of *Liber Apologeticus*, which equally is a demonstration of academic competence and intellectual exercise. Chaundler dedicated and sent the play to the Bishop of Bath and Wells, Bishop Bekynton, and this dedication dates the play as during Chaundler's first Chancellorship (i.e. about 1460) and suggests that the play itself, like the manuscript copy for the Bishop with its marginal summaries and fourteen illustrations, may have been designed merely to be read. However, the modern editor, Doris Enright-Clark-Shoukri, plausibly surmises that, since Chaundler was not one to hide his light under a bushel, and since the *Libellus* was read aloud, the play might have received some kind of performance, despite its lack of stage directions, or any reference to a theatre, even if it was only a public reading by students in the hall of New College.[13]

In *Liber Apologeticus* Chaundler covers the history of man and the scheme of redemption. He divides the material into four acts, which is in itself an important dramatic innovation; this is the earliest extant play in England to use such a clear structural separation of the different stages of man's history. Skelton has such a sense of the notional phases which the parts of the play represent, but the formal structure does not explicitly proclaim it as Chaundler's does. One could say that the idea of units forming an over-all design belongs more to the study play than to the practical theatre, perhaps, but it is a pleasure to the reader, and confirms the sort of structural pattern that one tends to distinguish in other plays such as *Wisdom* and *Mankind*. The ambitious range of subject-matter is thus broken down by the ground-plan into four aspects: I. Creation, Tempation and Fall; II. Responsibility and Guilt; III. Debate of the Daughters of God; IV. Death and Salvation. These subjects are treated by exposition in lengthy speeches (mainly for God and Man) and by the presentation of opposing arguments in dialogue. The main points of interest are as follows.

The play begins with an explanation by God of the fall of Lucifer and the creation of Man. God gives Man a symbolic orb and sceptre and mantle of immortality; he gives him also free will and two companions, Reason, as his guide, and Sensuality, as a beast of burden, with a warning not to taste Sensuality's forbidden fruits. Reason gives Man a mirror in which he may contemplate and understand his own nature. Man is then flattered and tempted by Sensuality, and, rejecting the advice of Reason and thereby wounding her, he tastes the forbidden fruit. Immediately sorrow and a sense of his vileness turn Man to lamentation, and in a passionate soliloquy, which ends the first act, he bewails the loss of his sceptre of justice and the golden orb. In the mirror of contemplation he sees his face as the image of death, and confronts his own deformity and confusion. He cries, 'Quo fugit decor meus, imago Dei in utriusque hominis vultu relucens?' (Whither has fled my beauty, the image of God, shining in the face of every man?), and realises that he has lost the mantle of immortality.[14]

Act II is a debate between God and Man concerning God's reasons for creating evil and the nature of free will. The central point is Man's question why God may not be declared the cause of man's sin, since he created man's free will, which is vividly compared to giving a man poison to quench his thirst. The main point of God's lengthy reply about the nature of freedom and virtue is that it would be impossible to have voluntary good without evil: 'Utrumque te posse volui, sed unum facere, bonum scilicet, quod et imperavi' (I wanted you to be capable of either, but to do one – the good, that is, which I also commanded).[15]

The material of Act III is the familiar heavenly debate or trial scene: in this version, with Justice and Truth acting as prosecution and Mercy and Peace as defence before God as judge of Man, the resolution of the debate comes through Peace's appeal to the unity of the sisters in God, and God's proposal of the Incarnation as a solution of the conflict between Justice and Mercy. The redemption is announced to Man and God teaches him through the parable of the Good Samaritan and commits him to the care of the four Cardinal Virtues, who will protect him against the Devil.

In Act IV Man's joy in his restoration, as Justice teaches him judgment, Temperance moderates his desires, Fortitude strengthens his will and Prudence warns him against the temptation of demons, is cut short by the hideous, threatening face of Fear of Death, who presents him with a letter from Death, in which he declares his lordship over all flesh. Man reads this letter out. (It is a good example of fifteenth-century epistolary style and ends resoundingly:

> Scriptum infra tartarea claustra, ministrante nobis specialissimo nostre secretario, Sathana, post annos regni nostri sexies mille sexcentos et viginti quatuor. [Written below the gates of Tartarus, with Satan, our most special secretary, ministering to us, in the year of our reign six times a thousand, six hundred and twenty-four.])[16]

In great doubt Man first accepts fear of death, because fear may usefully prepare for the coming of Death as a thief in the night, but then receives a second letter, brought by the messenger Charity from the fiery Seraphim, announcing the way of salvation and the joys of heaven. Man reads this letter too. (This is written 'in the most bright palace of the Lord God of Hosts, in the eternal reign without end and without beginning';[17] Chaundler finds in this convention of ending a letter a neat way of pointing God's freedom from time.) Man rejoices and the virtues drive out fear, which is revealed as a weapon in the hands of the powers of evil. Death himself appears to threaten Man, but Man dies joyfully; he is stripped of the flesh by Death, but Justice restores his mantle of immortality, Temperance his golden sceptre, Prudence the golden orb and Fortitude his beauty and glory. Finally Charity places a golden crown upon his head and bids the angels raise him to heaven.

Several things are obvious from an outline of the play. First, as Doris Enright-Clark-Shoukri says, it was 'conceived as a kind of dramatic debate and resembles the later closet or banquet dramas of Medwall, Rastell and Heywood'.[18] Secondly, it shares a number of themes and figures with English moral plays: the conflict of Reason and Sensuality within Man, the fall into sin brought by the exercise of free will, the debate of the Daughters of God, and the coming of Death are main themes which occur elsewhere. The use of allegorical personifications of Death and the Virtues, with the main figures of God and Man, makes the characters like those of the moral plays, though there is a major difference in the very minor part played by personified vice. This difference is one sign of Chaundler's separation of purpose from that of the writers of the theatre plays of the period: he did not have (or feel obliged to use) a *homiletic* purpose in writing, and so did not need to shape his material into an improving lesson. His purpose was to explain the ways of God to man in clear Latin prose, through an intelligent command of arguments about free will, etc. The temptation of man is presented as an assault on the mind rather than the senses (Sensuality exploits his pride in freedom, tempting him to explore its extent). It is striking that Chaundler's version of the debate of the Daughters of God does not mention the Crucifixion, nor place much stress on the sacraments; he presents a philosophical answer to the problem of sin in man. He is concerned with the unity of virtues in God, reconciliation and the compassion of God, and not with the purpose found in vernacular plays of satirising and reforming the worldly life of man in sin.

Despite differences, the comparison between *Liber Apologeticus* and *Wisdom* is interesting, and I think one can fairly see Chaundler's play as a more extreme form of the kind of drama that *Wisdom* represents. Both plays may be criticised as 'lacking in action and in appeal to the senses of the audience',[19] but Chaundler is even less interested in writing realistic dialogue than the author of *Wisdom* and he uses less stage business. He does make use, as *Wisdom* does, of appearance and physical objects as symbols to represent moral states: in the middle of the play Man is clad in a coat of the skins of dead animals (reminders of mortality) in place of the cloak of immortality, and furnished with a scourge to correct sensuality in place of the sceptre of justice, and, for the orb, which indicated lordship over the earth, he must substitute a spade, to remind him that he is of the earth and will return to dust, as well as to lead his life in toil. Man's symbols and his beauty are restored at the end, so that we return to symbolic pageantry to create a final tableau of apotheosis. In this last scene also, the use of messengers shows a sense of dramatic effect, and the returning of the gifts of God to Man one at a time by the Cardinal Virtues and Charity shows that Chaundler knew how to create a patterned ritual and a final picture.

A second area of comparison is the use of expository speeches. In *Liber Apologeticus* they are often very lengthy and completely static (even more so than the speeches of Wisdom in the Macro play), but they are interesting as argument, and occasionally, as in the impassioned rhetoric of Man's speech at the end of Act I, can be moving. The main appeal of the play is its ideas; it is an early example of the 'Don Juan in Hell' concept of drama and its best passages could appropriately be called Shavian. The interest of the ideas comes partly from the material used by Chaundler. Like the author of *Wisdom* he does not draw on the sermon-tradition of instruction and exhortation intended for a popular audience, but on the more meditative, philosophical kinds of Christian teaching such as those found in works written for religious orders. Both show a greater interest in ideas (but not theological ones, rather in concepts of the human mind and will) than other moral plays. The author of *Wisdom* drew on Hilton, Suso, St Bernard, Bonaventura and the school of Rolle for his first and last scenes, where Wisdom speaks of the soul, human nature, repentance and charity. Chaundler's sources are to some extent more scholastic, particularly in that his main authority (Peter Lombard's *Sentences*) is an academic Latin one, not the more emotional, vernacular, devotional works of his own time. But he adds to Lombard's argument in the first two acts material on the will from the more evocative and suggestive pen of Boethius. In Act III his main source is a sermon of St Bernard, but again there is influence from Boethius (the idea of the essential oneness of the Daughters of God), and Chaundler's use of Biblical quotation shows the influence of the *Charter of the Abbey of the Holy Ghost*, a devotional work in a learned manner, akin to material drawn on in *Wisdom*. In Act IV he draws on *De Anima* (whence Chaundler could have developed a dramatisation of the Battle between the Vices and the Virtues had he been interested); this work was a compilation – Book I by St Bernard, Book II attributed to Augustine but more probably by a twelfth-century Cistercian, Book III by either Bernard or Hugh of St Victor, who also possibly wrote Book IV. The tradition it represents was drawn on by many medieval works of devotion and meditation, such as *Sawles Warde*, and is part of the same current that runs through *Wisdom*.

This example of university drama shows that dialogue was an accepted literary mode in which a man of learning could display his knowledge of and interest in religious and philosophical ideas. There is some use of visual symbolism and the effective dramatic tableau, but, for the most part, Chaundler uses dramatic form simply as a rhetorical device. It represents one kind of academic influence upon fifteenth-century drama; it does not preclude others, and *Mankind* could be a representative of a very different university tradition. The main connecting-link between drama and academic philosophy was debate. Through the debate tradition of teaching and training theologians and lawyers, and the existence of works in Latin and in English translations in which ideas about man's nature, the purpose of his life on earth, the relationship between good and evil, and so on, were discussed, a learned drama could have been born. I suggest that *Liber Apologeticus* is one sign of this and *Wisdom* another. Further signs are to be seen in the use of debate and the drama of ideas within the cycles and within longer plays like *The Castle of Perseverance*.

In a number of places in the cycles pageants tend to turn into discussions of Christian philosophy, or, more often, into speeches of exposition: a full review of them would be a strong reminder of how many themes the cycles and the moral plays have in common. In the speeches given to God and Lucifer early in the cycles, given to the Old Testament patriarchs and prophets, given to John the Baptist, to 'Doctour' and 'Expositor', are many points of theory, of doctrine and of principle; these speeches and their expository nature are an obvious aspect of the didactic basis of medieval religious plays. But more significant are the places where, in some versions of the material, playwrights have taken opportunities to insert or to develop substantial argument. One instance is the treatment of *Christ and the Doctors* in the N-Town cycle. This was a theme for which the Bible provided no material beyond the idea that Christ amazed the learned doctors; in order to demonstrate Christ's precocious learning medieval dramatists had to make some attempt at an impression of intellectual skill and profound understanding. One way, found in Continental versions of the story, was to have Christ show how many of the Old Testament prophecies had been fulfilled. The way found in the English versions in the York, Towneley and Chester Cycles and the Coventry plays, which are all similar, is a less effective exposition by Christ of the Ten Commandments. In Play 21 of the N-Town cycle there is a much more striking rendering of the theme. The effectiveness comes partly from an attempt to characterise the doctors. The playwright makes them conform to the pattern of boastful pride leading to deserved humiliation; they are presented satirically in speeches listing all their branches of erudition and in their scornful dismissal of Christ, when he joins in their discourse, as a mere babe-in-arms who had better 'Goo hom and sytte in thi moderys lappe/And put a mokador apon thi brest'. This gives a lively touch to a potentially stilted pageant, but its real strength lies in the demonstration of Christ's wisdom. The dramatist's method is an exposition, by means of the powerful symbolism of the sun, of the Trinity and the Immaculate Conception, and a thematic emphasis on the Incarnation, which both shows its relationship to the sequence of events covered in the cycle up to that point, and prefigures the role that Christ is to fulfil. This is presented partly in terms of the opposition of Christ and the Devil, which is a distinctive feature (among the English Cycles) of the treatment of the Passion in the N-Town cycle. The pattern of the doctors' questions and Christ's answers works well to dramatise ideas, which serve both to instruct the audience in Christian doctrine and to emphasise the unifying threads which hold together the Old and New Testaments and the over-all scheme of the Cycle: Creation, Fall, Redemption and Judgment. At the same time the playwright has sufficient stage skill to add humour and feeling to the scene through the change in the doctors from pride to humble acceptance of Christ as their Master, and through Mary's anxiety for her child, which is imaginatively used to bring the pageant to a close with Christ's own humility in his moving acceptance of the need to give up his own will in order 'to plese my Modyr mylde'. This is a pageant in which the focus remains on the historical material, an important episode in the life of Christ, but where the dramatic interest of question and answer and of serious themes have been intelligently used to amplify and to give depth to the subject.

That represents one step towards the drama of ideas; a further one is found when the ideas are put into the mouths of personified virtues. Here again it is the N-Town cycle that provides the instance, in its use of the debate of the Daughters of God. This is placed before the Salutation and Conception (in Pageant 11) and opens with one of the prologues given in the Cycle to the figure called Contemplacio.[20] This figure functions in early appearances, as the figure of 'Doctour' or 'Expositor' elsewhere, simply to introduce or to explain. The prologue here is different. It is both a rhetorical expression of the sorrows of man since the Fall and of the hope of the coming of the Messiah, and also a passionate lyrical plea to God to

'Cum vesyte us in this tyme of nede'.

So Contemplacio becomes an allegorical figure involved in the drama, expressing the contrition of God's creatures and identifying himself as man contemplating his own history and nature, and not just a bookish explicator. In response to the plea, which is supported by angels, God the Father declares that 'Tyme is come of reconsyliacion', and the Cardinal Virtues are brought in, one by one, in reaction to the prospect of man's release from Hell.

The purpose of the debate of the four virtues, both in this play and elsewhere, was to examine God's treatment of man and in particular to relate God's judgment of Adam and Eve to the idea of redemption. In the pageant here it is used to lead to the Annunciation, so that the Incarnation is presented as God's response to man's sorrowful pleas and as the fulfilment of an inevitable pattern needed for the reconciliation of justice and mercy. The speeches of the virtues are quite short, but clear and forceful. In two 8-line stanzas, Truth points out the inconsistency of God if Adam is restored to bliss; Mercy responds in two equal stanzas, urging God to compassion for the souls in Hell and praying him:

That helle hounde, that hateth the, byddyth hym, 'Ho!'
Thi love, man, no lengere lete hym kepe.   (87–8)

Justice's two stanzas remind Mercy that man chose the Devil as his master and therefore:

Xulde he be savyd? Nay, nay, nay.   (96)

After an intervening 1-stanza speech by Mercy, describing Justice as too vengeful, Peace completes the pattern with two stanzas urging that the sisters join in submission to God's judgment, which, in symmetrical short speeches, they then do. God the Son, in His dual role of Wisdom and Redeemer, explains the need, if the virtues are to survive, of another death, of one sinless so that Hell may not hold him. The voices of the virtues are used to express the strength of love that would be needed to suffer death for man, and to affirm that only Christ himself is capable of it. Christ asks how he may don the clothing of manhood and the third person of the Trinity speaks as the power which can effect it:

I, love, to your lover xal yow lede.   (183)

In Mercy's last speech, the sisters are reconciled and kiss, and Father, Son and Holy Ghost prepare Gabriel for the task of the Annunciation.

The scene is powerful, bold in its use of the three persons of the Trinity in the manner of allegorical figures, moving in its expression of God's love for man, and ingenious in its weaving together of the theme of man's sorrow, the debate about justice, and the next stage in the Scriptural narrative. The debate itself is short and formal, with symmetrical speeches making us more conscious of the pattern than of passionate, crucial or tough argument. The three persons of God make another part of the pattern, and from the heightened emotional appeal of the prologue, the dramatist develops a skilful, stylised presentation of central ideas and feelings of the Christian faith. The interest of argument has been subordinated to the 'historical' aspect of the cycle, but the ideas have been strikingly put into the hearer's mind.

The passage from Psalm 85 (verse 10) 'Mercy and truth are met together; righteousness and peace have kissed one another', which was the origin of the motif of the debate of the Daughters of God, is one of the few places in Scripture which uses this kind of personification of ideas. It was a basic text from which medieval commentators could justify reading Scripture in allegorical terms; this perhaps explains why the theme turns up in so many places. It is found in Hugh of St Victor, St Bernard, Grosseteste and Bonaventura, all influential sources for vernacular writers. It is in *Vices and Virtues*, *Sawles Warde* and *Cursor Mundi*. Langland uses it in Passus XVIII of *Piers Plowman*, Lydgate in *The Life of Our Lady*, and it provides the material for the first book of the fifteenth-century encyclopaedic, didactic poem *The Court of Sapience*.[21]

It appears in three fifteenth-century plays written in England, *Liber Apologeticus*, the N-Town cycle, Play 11 and *The Castle of Perseverance*. It was thus a meeting-place, in a sense, of different literary genres, a reminder that themes and the debate-form in dialogue are shared by drama, dream poems, prose allegories, etc. There are many variations in the use to which it was put in different contexts. Hope Traver linked the versions in *The Castle of Perseverance* and the N-Town cycle as showing the influence of the *Meditationes Vitae Christi* (formerly attributed to Bonaventura), whereas Chaundler's version is closer to St Bernard.[22] But it seems more significant that the N-Town cycle uses the debate in a way which is similar to that of Langland, though at a different point. Langland places it after the Crucifixion, and the debate leads into the majestic scene of Christ's confrontation with Satan at the gates of Hell, after which the daughters are reconciled. Though the Harrowing of Hell gives to the debate a very different emphasis from that of the play, the effect in the two is similar in that the speeches of the personified virtues are woven in with the narrative of God's actions and the moving expression of God's love for man. The stress is on God's deeds and speeches and the *enacting* of the Redemption: the discussion of justice and mercy is used to give depth and theory to this, rather than as an abstract discussion of law and ethics for the sake of philosophy, theology or doctrine. There is a contrast both in *Liber Apologeticus* and *The Castle of Perseverance*. In the former the scene is presented as the trial of man after his fall, with God as judge, and the opposing views are given a court-room sense of alternation of point and counter-point; here there is a greater interest in actual argument, such as that Justice is constant and perpetual and that God will contradict its very essence if he starts being flexible, or that Mercy is useless as an abstract idea and can only justify existing if put into practice. The ideas are familiar, but the extent of the expression of them gives them more weight. God's announcement of the Incarnation is led up to through the idea of the unity of the sisters and the underlying meaning of that unity that God himself is all of them. In *The Castle of Perseverance* the speeches begin in response to Anima's cry for help at the hour of Mankind's death and the condemnation of his soul, but they have not even such strength of feeling as is found in the N-Town cycle. The debate brings the play to a close in lengthy formal speeches in elaborately decorative stanzas. The effect is of a set of literary lyrics about the life of man: for example, Truth says that man shall pay because of his good fortune and his ingratitude:

> For man on molde halt welthe and wele,
> Lust and lykynge in al hys lyfe,
> Techynge, prechynge, in every sele.
> But he forgetyth the Lord belyve.
> Hye of hert, happe and hele,
> Gold and sylvyr, chyld and wyf,
> Denteth drynke at mete and mele.
> Unnethe the to thanke he can not kyth
> In any maner thynge.   (3288–96)

This is poetry in the manner of the Vernon lyrics – thoughtful and just, quite effectively pointed in expression in a short extract, but at length diffuse, slack, lacking the real bite either of emotion or of intellectual argument. In this style the patterned exchange of pleas proceeds, identifying *The Castle of Perseverance* as a static type of drama, using figures as talking masks. The scene is less effective as theatre than the N-Town cycle and less effective as argument than Chaundler's Latin.

If we now return to *Wisdom*, I hope that it is apparent that in a variety of plays, and with differences of tone and emphasis, one can find parallels to the handling in *Wisdom* of religious concepts, and to the creation of scenes out of demonstrations of the wisdom of God. In these demonstrations recurring themes are the love between God and the soul, man's free will and the consequences of his exercise of it, and the theoretical justification for the Incarnation. Though *Wisdom* does not use the debate of the Daughters of God, the dramatic idea in the scene in the N-Town cycle, Play 11 has much in common with the Macro play – in the emphasis on God's fervent love for man, in the use of the three persons of the Trinity (present in *Wisdom* both in Wisdom himself and his exposition of his role, and reflected in the three powers of the human soul), in the symmetry of the speeches, in Contemplacio's prologue and the speeches of Anima expressing man's desire to be freed from sorrow, to be cleansed and to be united with God, and in the numerical patterning. The differences come from *Wisdom*'s pageant-like qualities (symbolic pictures, dance, etc.), as well as the different subject-matter in the central scenes.

Thus, I suggest that a major aspect of *Wisdom* is that it is part of a tradition of drama of Christian ideas, which overlaps with other forms of writing, such as moral allegories in verse and prose, which also use debate and dialogue as rhetorical devices. Among the plays that use debate, or that introduce theoretical discussion, one can see some variation of treatment and use. One could add others to the plays I have mentioned (such as the pageants dealing with Satan's temptations of Christ), but here the range is displayed. There is more similarity between *Wisdom* and the N-Town cycle pageant than there is among the three moral plays, even though they overlap and belong together. Chaundler's *Liber Apologeticus* shows us a more bookish university debate, which can hold the attention by the interest of the material, despite the stilted use of the dramatic form. In *The Castle of Perseverance* one finds more of an empty display of attitudes, though these are stylishly expressed. *Wisdom* and the N-Town cycle combine intense feeling (drawing on a similar devotional tradition) with formal stylisation and symmetry in the speeches and numerical patterning in the arrangement of the figures.

3. *Pageants, Mummings and Masques*

In *Wisdom* there are three elements which connect the play with the forms of pageantry and court entertainment from which the later masque grew: first, the use of elaborate costume; secondly, the use of non-speaking actors in allegorical tableaux and dances; and, thirdly, the use of the characters, speaking and non-speaking, in processions, stage patterns and other symbolic stage effects. There are several possible sources for each and all of these; it would take me too far away from my subject to attempt a survey of them and I do no more here than touch on a few of the relevant points.

The 'disguisings' performed by the Gentlemen of the Chapel Royal in Westminster Hall as part of the celebrations of the marriage of Prince Arthur, eldest son of Henry VII, to Katherine of Aragon in 1501 are a famous instance of costumed tableaux appearing on moving waggons ('pagens proper and subtil').[23] On one was a castle, with ladies within and children singing on the turrets; the second bore a ship, whence came Hope and Desire to sue, unsuccessfully, for the Ladies' favour on behalf of the Knights of the Mount of Love; the third bore the Mount itself, from which eight knights in disguise issued, assaulted the castle, won the ladies and joined them in dancing. It is a short step from such celebratory pageantry to the masque, which is first identified under that name in Hall's *Chronicle*, where Henry VIII is described as appearing (in 1512) disguised, with eleven others, 'after the maner of Italie, called a maske', and inviting ladies of the court to join in the dance. Christmas revels and tournament games at court at a much earlier date made use of elaborate, lavish disguises, such as masks with golden beards and animal costumes. The accounts of the Royal Wardrobe of the court of Edward III record costumes for games as early as 1347, and it was at the court of Charles VI of France in 1393 that the tragic incident described by Froissart occurred, in which five nobles of the court disguised as wild men had their costumes set on fire and died of the burns. The descriptions in *Wisdom* of the three groups of dancers who appear as followers of the corrupted powers of man could easily occur in such chronicle accounts of actual court revels, though their function is different, since they occur as part of a staged play with dialogue.

A reminder that the word 'pageant' has several meanings is provided by other connections with the play. The symbolic processions, the exorcising of the demons and Anima's singing in the manner of the lamentations of Passion Week are reminders of the liturgical strain in medieval drama, and of the existence of such combinations of religious and dramatic activities as is found in the Pageant of the Purification performed by the Guild of St Mary at Beverley (founded in 1355). When the members of the guild processed, with 'music and gladness', to church on the Feast of the Purification of the Virgin, one of the members was dressed as Mary, carrying a representation of the baby Jesus in her arms; others were arrayed as Joseph, Simeon and two angels, who carried candelabra. The pageant Virgin offered her son to Simeon and the brothers and sisters of the guild offered their wax lights and a penny each.[24]

Yet another aspect of the 'pageant' (from Latin *pagina*, 'page', 'paragraph', used with reference to scholastic drama) is found in Lydgate's *A Pageant of Knowledge*, an enumeration of the estates of society, the seven types of wisdom, the seven founders of the artificial sciences, the seven liberal arts and their founders, the planets and the signs of the zodiac, the four elements, the four temperaments, the four seasons and the mutability of the world.[25] The various pageants of which this work is composed are derived from Ausonius and belong to an idea of poetry as educational and mnemonic. There is no indication that the verses accompanied a tableau or dumb-show, but the second stanza is attributed to separate speakers and could provide the basis of a staged version of such a display of ranks, attributes and faculties:

Pryncys   To us longeth prestys to governe.

Presthode   And we be bounde to lyve in parfytnes.

Juges   Betwene ryght and wrong our office doth dyscerne.

Merchantes   In bying and sellyng we shall do no falsnes.

Knyghthode   We shall defende trouthe and ryghtwysnes.

Plowman   Our occupacion to tyll and sowe the lond.

Werkemen   And by our labour we voyden idylnes.

Rycheman   We delyver our almes with our hond.

                                                    (9–16)

This is half-way between Lydgate's straightforward didactic poems and the more ambitious semi-dramatic works usually called 'mummings'. It is a reminder of fifteenth-century interest in educational literature and of the typical presentation of things in sets, often linked by numbers (7 and 4 here). The third scene of *Wisdom* is, in part, a more developed 'pageant' of this type, a series of sets of worldly vices.

Lydgate's *Mummings* themselves have been fully described and examined by Schirmer, Pearsall, Wickham and others.[26] There are seven of them and they consist of verses to accompany dumb-shows presented on some court occasion or for some civic function. The most interesting aspect of them in relationship to *Wisdom* is that the role of the poet or narrator in some of the *Mummings* (eg. *A Mumming at Eltham* [1424] and *A Mumming for the Mercers of London* [probably 1429]) is that of demonstrator, who points to the non-speaking allegorical figures and explains their significance. This 'master of the dumb-show' effect is used by the playwright in *Wisdom* when Mind, Understanding and Will introduce their retinues and identify them one by one. The same idea is further developed in the scene where Wisdom explains the significance of Anima's costume. The Lydgate pageant nearest to a moral play is *A Mumming at London* (1427), which is identified as 'a desguysing tofore the gret estates of this lande' and which consists of an allegorical masque of Fortune and the Four Cardinal Virtues. Dame Fortune enters first and is the occasion for an exposition of mutability; the four other Dames, Prudence, Righteousness, Fortitude (or Magnificence) and Temperance, are presented as our protectors against Fortune's fickleness, and described in turn, before they are instructed by the explicator to close the pageant with a song around the fire. Like *A Pageant of Knowledge*, this is based on Ausonius and is in the literary, ample, moralistic style of Lydgate's other allegorical works such as *Resoun and Sensuallyte*. However, though the personifications, the themes and the didacticism link it with plays of the fifteenth century, there is no dramatic quality about it. The only one of the *Mummings* to attempt a dramatic effect is *A Mumming at Hertford*, performed at Hertford Castle, probably in 1430 before Henry VI, then aged nine, and an audience of the nobility. For the pleasure of aristocrats, Lydgate here attempted a more popular vein, and presented a kind of debate between husbands of 'the rude upplandishe people' and their wives, with the wives' answer written in direct speech, as if 'performed'. The husbands' case is presented in the narrator's voice as a petition to the king and is enlivened by some comic names (Robin, or Hob, the Reeve complains of his wife Beatrice Bittersweet and Colin the Cobbler of his, Cicely Sour-Cheer) and touches of 'low-life' satire, which show the influence of Chaucer's Wife of Bath. This rather laboured effort (it is difficult to see a justification for Schirmer's description of it as 'This lively play, reminiscent of a Renaissance farce', except that it is a degree less leaden than the other *Mummings*) is important as a bridge between the dumb-show with explanatory commentary and the tableau with dialogue.

One last thread connecting the masque-like aspects of *Wisdom* with other drama leads again to the N-Town cycle. In the Passion Plays there (which show evidence both of being originally two self-contained plays and of an origin in Continental Passion Plays), one finds far more elaborate stage-directions than are used elsewhere in the surviving texts of Corpus Christi Cycles, and also the only instances of the use of dumb-show in the cycles.[27] The unusual degree of detail about costume and an indication of the richness sometimes available is apparent in:

> Here xal Annas shewyn hymself in his stage beseyn after a busshop of the hoold lawe in a scarlet gowne; and over that a blew tabbard furryd with whyte and a mytere on his hed after the hoold lawe; ij doctorys stondyng by hym in furryd hodys and on beforn hem with his staff of Astat and eche of hem on here hedys a furryd cappe with a gret knop in the crowne and on stondyng beforn as a sarazyn the which xal be his masangere.   (N-Town cycle, Play 26)

Dumb-show is indicated most strikingly in the direction at the beginning of the scene with Pilate's wife. After a lengthy introduction for Satan, we are told:

> Here xal the devyl gon to Pylatys wyf; the corteyn drawyn as she lyth in bedde and he xal no dene make but she xal, sone after that he is come in, makyn a rewly noyse, comyng and rennyng of the schaffald and here shert, and here kyrtyl in here hand, and sche xal come befor Pylat leke a mad woman, seyng thus . . .

> (N-Town cycle, Play 31)

The emphasis on appearance and the realisation of the dramatic possibilities of mime indicated in such directions are evidence both of sophistication in dramatist and audience and of some luxury of presentation. *Wisdom* and the N-Town cycle share the studied quality which comes from the use of a fixed stage; the dramatist has composed in terms of stage pictures, and they are pictures of a more elaborate and complex kind than were possible within the limits of the moving waggon.

From the different strands which I have tried to indicate briefly it is possible to weave a background for the pageant-like aspects of *Wisdom*. The play draws on existing and developing forms of allegorical masque and liturgical and literary pageant. The N-Town cycle shows some of the same features in its Passion sequence, just as it shows some of *Wisdom*'s interest in the exposition of religious ideas. *Wisdom* is more readily understood against this background than as part of some idea of 'morality play', which tends to link *Wisdom* with plays with which it has in common only the Devil and some aspects of the depiction of worldly vice. The non-realistic aspects of medieval drama have often been ignored, or dismissed as the stilted, unimaginative traits which had to be replaced by comedy and realism, but medieval drama can be effective as ritual, pattern and picture. Sometimes, as in *Wisdom*, plays can by the use of these features be more effective than the common run of medieval dramas, whose weakness is apt to be verbal weakness; those plays which depend least on words and most on shapes, symbols, costumes, symbolic appearances, music, dance, and the representation of ideas through figures and emblems are often creative and imaginative. In the cycles the playwrights rely on symbol and tableau to convey the majesty of God, the awesome mystery of Creation and the solemnity of Judgment, among other things, but it is difficult to assess the over-all importance of visual appearances, music and so on, except where the text survives with detailed descriptions and instructions to the players.

One can be more sure about the 'drama of ideas' aspect of *Wisdom*, since the debate becomes a type of Tudor play, and *Wisdom* can be seen as an ancestor of later university and humanist drama, at least as far as the assumption that an audience could be interested by intellectual distinctions among the different faculties of man. Whether the plays of Heywood, for instance, develop from *Wisdom* is a matter of less importance, though, than the recognition that this Macro play (or this Digby play) is distinct from the others, more abstract, intellectual and picturesque, more deeply felt and having the power to penetrate more sharply, through symbolism and argument, into the nature and state of the soul.

CHAPTER FIVE

The Castle of Perseverance
and the Long Play

1.   *The Castle of Perseverance*

The Castle of Perseverance is often given pride of place in discussions of the medieval moral plays for three reasons. First, it was probably composed in the first quarter of the fifteenth century and is therefore the earliest complete allegorical play in English. Secondly, it is a good starting-point for discussion of the subject-matter of moral drama, since it includes all the main themes and figures found in medieval allegorical plays. Thirdly, the famous drawing in the Macro manuscript of the castle in the centre of the circle formed by a ditch, surrounded by five scaffolds allotted to God (west), Flesh (south), World (east), Devil (north) and Covetousness (north-east), has been the main stimulus to discussion of the staging of single plays in the medieval period, especially to consideration of the possibility of 'theatre-in-the-round'.[1] Thus historical importance has subordinated the other Macro plays and *The Castle of Perseverance* has, by implication, been credited with greater achievement than its dramatic power actually warrants. It lacks the flexibility of tone, especially in the use of satire and colloquialism, of *Mankind* and later moral plays; its all-inclusiveness has the disadvantage of great length (3649 lines); its ambitious staging gives a ponderous deliberation to the actions and movements of the play. But the main reason for its lack of effectiveness, in comparison with *Everyman*, for instance, is its poetic technique: the use of alliteration as the main way of heightening the style slows the expression by encouraging a flourish of redundant words, and even more diffuse is the composition of speeches in stanza-units (mainly 13-line stanzas, varied with 9-line ones and some less frequent quatrains) which are, at many points, arranged with a greater degree of symmetry than even in *Wisdom*. There is very little dialogue in the play, as a result; for the most part characters do not converse as much as elocute and expatiate alternately. This poetic amplitude is typical of the earlier fifteenth century; it is parallel to (and not, as the other plays are, a subsequent development of) the move towards comprehensiveness and encyclopaedic didacticism visible in Lydgate's work. Just as the scope of the subject-matter makes the play similar to such pieces of moral thoroughness as *The Pilgrimage of the Life of Man*, so the verbal amplitude resembles Lydgate's expansive, decorative and rhetorical expression of moral ideas. Though a dramatic weakness, if we consider the play in terms of the entertainment it offers, the comprehensive scope is the feature of *The Castle of Perseverance* which distinguishes it as a type of drama; the scale, the range of subject-matter and the correspondingly expansive manner make this an example of 'epic' theatre.

The epic intention manifests itself in a number of ways. First, the playwright covers not only the life of man on earth but he begins the play before man's birth and ends the play after his death. At the beginning we are made aware of the plot to destroy Mankind (Humanum Genus) in parallel declarative speeches by World (Mundus), Devil (Belyal) and Flesh (Caro); in heavily alliterating verse the battle-lines are drawn up by an assignment of sins – Covetousness as the World's treasurer, Pride, Envy and Wrath as the Devil's allies and Gluttony, Lechery and Sloth as Flesh's tools. Then we are presented with the new-born Mankind, naked, ignorant and helpless. Similarly, but in reverse order, at the end of the play, Mankind dies, equally helpless, bewildered and stripped of his possessions, and his fate is then discussed by superhuman powers; in equally patterned poetic ritual the four daughters of God assess the state of Mankind's soul and submit their case to the judgment of God, whose rescue of Anima from the Bad Angel brings the play to an end. It is thus the playwright's intention to present the whole case of man's life set between the forces of evil and of good and to show human life as part of the contest between the Divine and the demonic powers. The rivalry of Belyal and God is represented as a struggle for power, and both, at appropriate moments, claim over-lordship. So Belyal on his first appearance boasts of his command over great men:

> Kyngys, kayserys, and kempys and many a kene knyth,
> These lovely lordys han lernyd hem my lawe.
> To my dene thei wyl drawe.   (215–7)

When God appears at the end, it is not only as judge that He speaks, but also as victor in the contest for that same power:

> Kyng, kayser, knyt and kampyoun,
> Pope, patriark, prest, and prelat in pes,
> Duke dowtyest in dede, be dale and be doun,
> Lytyl and mekyl, the more and the les,
> All the statys of the werld is at myn renoun;
> To me schal thei yeve acompt at my dygne des.   (3611–6)

The intention is ambitious in style as well as comprehensive in range of material. The poetic style is elevated and aspires at times to grandeur, and there is a kind of grand obviousness about the figures and ideas. Characters say (sometimes at length) just what one would expect, and this, though it risks and does not avoid falling into platitude, also gives to *The Castle of Perseverance* a sense of solidity and centrality.

A second epic aspect is the treatment of the contest between good and evil in terms of actual physical battle, with a full-scale encounter between the Seven Deadly Sins and the Seven Virtues as a central set-piece. *The Castle of Perseverance* is the only medieval allegorical play to treat the moral life of man in the terms used in the *Psychomachia* of Prudentius, though this early medieval Latin poet (fl.400) is often invoked as the ancestor of the morality play in general.[2] With some knowledge of Virgil and of the epic tradition Prudentius expressed the Pauline idea of Christian battle against the powers of evil in a series of allegorical encounters, often picturesque and poetically suggestive. For instance, *Luxuria* is depicted in a golden chariot, scattering violets and rose petals over the virtues, who are faltering, tired after battle; *Sobrietas* rallies them and thrusts the Cross at Luxuria's horses, which bolt and cast her into the dust where she is put to the sword. After this episode *Avaritia*, warned by her sisters' defeat, employs guile and disguises herself by assuming the humble, homely appearance and behaviour of Thrift, in order to seduce and demoralise the virtues; she meets her match in *Operatio* (Good Works). It is from such heroic treatment of the conflicts within man's nature, and from the familiar medieval image of the besieged allegorical fortress (also going back to Prudentius who used the metaphor in his treatment of the origin of sin in the *Hamartigenia*) that the author of *The Castle of Perseverance* derived his grandest and most elevated scenes (Scenes XIII–XVIII).[3] This part of the play occurs after Mankind has repented of his sinful life and entered the Castle in a mood of resolution:

> The sevene synnys I forsake,
> And to these sevene vertuis I me take.   (1690–91)

In response Bad Angel sends Backbiter (*Detraccio*) as messenger to tell World, Flesh and Devil of Mankind's defection and to call them to battle. In scenes of detailed parallelism (XIII–XV) the playwright builds up to battle, weaving a pattern from Backbiter's demonic glee in dissension as he greets the three in turn and the fury of Belyal, the Flesh and the World with the sins who have failed to keep Mankind in sin; they rant and rave in the tyrant manner and beat the sins in reproof. Only Covetousness retains determination to defeat Mankind and bring him from the Castle:

> I schal do Mankynd come out fre,
> He schal forsake, as thou schalt se,
> The fayre vertus all.   (1874–6)

The World decrees the siege of the Castle and is identified as the most powerful of Mankind's adversaries:

> Ther schal no vertus dwellyn in my londe.   (1889)

and:

> I am the Werld. It is my wyll
> The Castel of Vertu for to spyll.   (1895–6)

Thus war is preceded by the councils of the enemy and these lead, in true epic style, to the preparations and declarations preliminary to battle. First Belyal bids the World, Covetousness and Folly to be ready for battle and Pride, in the role of banner-bearer, boasts, as is proper to his allegorical nature but also part of the necessary ritual of literary warfare. Then Flesh similarly exhorts and boasts, with alliterative rant, and they descend from their scaffolds to the *platea* for the battle itself. This occupies the long Scene XVIII (1969–2699) and is composed, after opening exhortations from the Bad and the Good Angels to their respective allies, of a series of encounters. First, the Devil's trio are brought in and, after a patterned series of speeches of vicious threat and staunch virtuous resistance, they fight; the sins are in turn defeated, Pride beaten down by Humility but Envy and Anger by unexpectedly vivid symbolic weapons, the roses of Charity and Patience, which stand for the Crucifixion, the blood of Christ and the beauty of virtue, among other things. Then come the three sins of the Flesh and the earlier pattern of scurrilous threats from the sin countered by resolution by the virtue is maintained by Gluttony versus Abstinence, Lechery versus Chastity and Sloth versus Business; again, fighting, victory for the virtues and lamentation by evil (here the Bad Angel) follow. Lastly come the World and his sin, Covetousness; he too has his one stanza of threat, countered by two stanzas from Generosity, as with the other meetings, but then the pattern changes. Covetousness continues and lures Mankind, who is growing 'hory and olde' and needs guidance, by tempting speeches in a substantial dialogue of alternate stanzas (2466–2543). Mankind succumbs and leaves the Castle. So the scene ends not in victory but in defeat for the virtues, with the Good Angel's sorrow and pleas for help. In this moment of defeat the Virtues state one of the central themes of moral drama – that Mankind has free will and, if he chooses to be a fool, then he may, and will pay for it later. As Mankind speaks of avarice ('Penyman is mekyl in mynde', 2665), the Good Angel laments and the World triumphs.

It is in this episode that one can best see the justification for the ambitious staging of *The Castle of Perseverance* and the working of the large-scale, patterned treatment of virtue and vice. The sense of comprehensiveness in the play depends on the visualisation of the whole play-area as the framework for the dramatic enactment of universal ideas; the action is seen as a whole shape or pattern, held together by the circle in the centre of the surrounding scaffolds. It is not just a matter of the playwright's clever technical use of different spaces, but rather the creation of a symbolic arena. The play-area represents the human mind, since this is the human space in which being occurs. But simultaneously it is a larger, cosmic area in which the ways of the world and the opposing abstract and supernatural forces act out their rivalry. The micro/macro-cosmic quality of the staging of the play means that movement within the stage area has both psychological and moral significance. The battle-scene effectively uses the possibilities created by the staging and by the literary tradition of the *Psychomachia*. The encounters are elevated by the symmetry rather than diminished; a stylised dance of battle is enacted as much in the rhetoric of the speeches as in the actions themselves. It is here too that one finds the playwright's most imaginative use of symbol, in the roses, symbols of Christ's Passion, which are the weapons of Charity and Patience. In that image and the creation of a grandiose and meaningful stage panorama the author of *The Castle of Perseverance* achieves greater theatrical and allegorical ambitions than are present in the minds of the authors of *Wisdom*, *Mankind* and the other moral plays.

But that is not true of the whole play. Less successful is the attempt at comprehensiveness that comes from the combination of themes and motifs, the doubling of moral actions, the large span of time and the very large number of characters and scenes. This represents not so much the epic writer's ambition to treat human life in terms of elevated heroic encounters of supernatural forces, as the chronicler's thoroughness, which takes on the progress of the pilgrimage of man's life through the world, through the Ages of Man. The episode of the Virtues, the Castle and the Battle is only one of the five main phases into which the play may be divided. Before that come: I. the powers in opposition to Mankind and his beginning; II. the taking on of sin; and III. recovery. After the battle comes: V. Old Age, Death and the fate of the soul. In this succession of themes and ages there is a mixture of effects and a varying standard of effectiveness.

In the early phases of the play the dramatist spends a lot of time establishing the figures and situation. The World, Belyal and the Flesh begin with heavily alliterative speeches in 13-line stanzas, expressing, from their several scaffolds, their natures and attitudes in turn; they are succeeded by Mankind (*Humanum Genus*) and the Good and Evil Angels, who also express a series of attitudes in the stilted manner of frozen tableau. Though Mankind is in doubt:

> I wolde be ryche in gret aray
> And fayn I wolde my sawle save,
> As wynde in watyr I wave. (377–9)

there is no interest on the writer's part in conveying dilemma or the painful wrestling between contending impulses in the soul; he is merely identifying the instability of man and the equal poise of his position between the Good and Evil Angels. His succumbing to the idea of being 'a mery man on molde' is arbitrary. Again with the third tableau (Scene V) of this first phase, the dramatist first presents a set of attitude-speeches, as the World appears with *Voluptas* (Lust and Liking) and *Stultitia* (Folly), and then begins to set his machinery of the scaffold-and-*platea* staging into operation. It proves very cumbersome. Lust and Liking and Folly have to descend to the acting circle to encounter the Bad Angel bringing news of Mankind, and then take him up to repeat it all to the World, who then instructs his two henchmen to dress Mankind in worldly robes, etc. Whereas in the battle scene the different areas provided by the scaffolds and the *platea* convey a sense of scale, and the preparations for battle build up suspense and significance, at the beginning of the play the ascents and descents and the carrying of messages from one figure to another in different parts of the set add an appalling laboriousness to the action. The allegorical business is made to seem unnecessarily portentous and this is, as I said earlier, added to by the static nature of the speeches and by each character's speeches being in stanza-units. The playwright does vary these from 13 lines to 9 lines and occasionally to quatrains, and in a few places changes the metre, as at the end of Scene V, where the World's instructions to Lust and Liking and Folly and their answers are expressed in shorter, brisker lines:

Voluptas In lyckynge and lust
　　　　　He schal rust
　　　　　Tyl dethys dust
　　　　　Do hym to day.   (635–9)

The handling of Mankind's assumption of sin (the second phase of the play, Scenes VI – half-way through XI, lines 647–1259) is similar. Its basis is a gallery of personifications, such as are found in *Le Roman de la Rose* and other vision-poems about dreamers' encounters with either the psychological abstractions of the love-allegory or the moral abstractions of the didactic allegory about sin and penitence. These personifications identify their natures in a series of declarative speeches. These contain some vivid expression of moral states, such as is found in the speech of Backbiter (*Detraccio*) at the beginning of Scene VI:

　　　　　To (*two* may not togedyr stonde
　　　　　But I Bakbyter be the thyrde.   (675–6)

But this speech, like many others in the play, is a static monologue, 'dramatic' only in the honorary sense of other dramatic monologues in that direct speech is used. The formal quality of the expression is increased by the patterned arrangement of the speeches, which is particularly marked in the treatment of the sins. After Covetousness has found Mankind an apt pupil, he calls on the other sins in the two groups of three used elsewhere: the Devil's three sins, Pride, Wrath and Envy, declare their nature in one stanza each and the Devil sends them off with a blessing; the performance is then repeated with the three sins of the Flesh. The laborious machinery of messengers and movements from scaffold to *platea* means that when the six sins all meet in the same place, they then repeat what they have already said, with variations, in the elaborate and lengthy ritual of Mankind's acceptance of each sin in turn. So Pride, Anger, Envy, Gluttony, Lechery and Sloth offer themselves to Mankind and to each Mankind speaks a stanza of acceptance; the ritual is completed by one of the few uses in the play of split stanzas as the Sin and Mankind express allegiance in two lines apiece:

> *Superbia*   I thi bowre to abyde
>   I com to dwelle be thi syde.
>
> *Humanum Genus* Mankynde and Pride
>   Sold dwell togedyr every tyde. (1084–7)

As I hope I made clear in my discussion of *Wisdom*, static tableau can be an effective way of staging moral ideas. In a sense *The Castle of Perseverance* begins in the manner of *Wisdom* by spending a long time explaining, demonstrating, and illustrating attitudes and creating patterns out of speeches and figures. But the dramatist has neither the skill in composition of stage pictures nor in the intelligent expression of religious ideas and feelings. The patterns come across as rigid, the speeches as rhetorical without oratory, the scenes as stolid, official representations of familiar moral matter. In the third phase of the play (the recovery of Mankind from sin, lines 1260–1601), there are, unexpectedly, flashes of powerful dramatic action (especially in the moment when Penitence inserts the spear of Penance in Mankind's heart) and some genuine dialogue (in the overcoming by Confession of the sinfulness of Mankind), but it is only with the battle between the virtues and the vices and the allegory of the Castle itself that the dramatist's methods seem to justify themselves. In the early scenes one sees the other, less appealing, aspect of the dramatist's large-scale ambitions – the dogged, comprehensive representation of the early phases of man's life and of the worldly vices and the sins who are his enemies. What the author of this 'most inclusive morality' is doing is pursuing a course partly derived from and more suited to narrative poetry; the early part, at least, 'may be read as an imitation of the action of life's pilgrimage as that action was formulated in a number of allegorical poems written during the late Middle Ages', especially in Deguileville's *Le Pèlèrinage de la Vie Humaine*.[4] Thus the largescale nature of *The Castle of Perseverance* is in some senses a representation of movements towards religious epic (which makes the play parallel to the Corpus Christi cycles), but in another way it is simply a staged version of the chronicle of an allegorical journey onto which the compendium of sins has been grafted.

Yet, when it comes to the siege of the Castle and the battle between virtues and vices, the large cast of personifications comes to have a weight and impressiveness which draws on the earlier establishment of themes and identities, tedious and stilted as this process was at the time. Eventually the play's obviousness commands respect, as large, solid works sometimes can, and it ends better than it began. The last phase of the play, the coming of Death, is powerful and imaginative. The World's fickleness and vengeful pettiness is what Mankind discovers as Death threatens, and the unreliability of the world and of possession is dramatised skilfully through the figure of *Garcio*, the anonymous boy sent by the World to inherit Mankind's possessions. Mankind's bewildered questions:

> What art thou? What woldyst thou mene? . . .
> What dost thou here? What woldyst thou have?   (2926, 2932)

are met by the terrifying answer:

> I am com to have al that thou hast,
> Poundys, parkys, and every place.   (2934–5)

Mankind's protests lead to a growth in the power of the usurper's voice:

> Deye on, for I am maystyr here.   (2963)

Eventually the boy's identity is revealed, producing neat irony from the possibilities of personification:

Humanum Genus I preye the now, syn thou this good schalt gete,
Telle thi name or that I goo.

Garcio
Loke that thou it not foryete:
My name is I Wot Nevere Whoo.   (2966–8)

This scene is one of the few places in medieval moral drama where the playwright manages to convey not just the lesson of the vanity of the world but the bitter experience of learning it. After Mankind's death, didacticism and a formal and symmetrical version of the debate of the Daughters of God bring the play to a close in judgment. The voice of God ends the play with a grandeur and authority appropriate to the ample scale and elevated aims of what has gone before.

The Castle of Perseverance requires consideration as a type of drama different from *The Pride of Life* and from the two other Macro plays, despite common ideas and themes, mainly because of its length and the different aspects of treatment which bring that scale about: the signs of 'epic' design in the treatment of supernatural warfare, the elevated style, etc.; the chronicling of the stages of man's life; the large-scale elaborate imagining of the stage-setting and the spectacular use of it in the battle-scene; and the combination of several different themes and moods which makes the play a typical medieval medley-series. The relationship between *The Castle of Perseverance* and the shorter moral plays is similar to that between Malory's *Morte D'Arthur* and the shorter Arthurian romances, such as *Sir Gawain and the Green Knight*; though the two Arthurian works have a common background, one is a full-scale chronicle of events from beginning to end, rising to heights of tragedy and of epic grandeur in its climax, whereas the other is an episode, telling of a particular adventure which illustrates the aspects of chivalry which the poet has found most worth exploring. There is not the same degree of difference in the case of the moral plays, but there is the same kind of difference. Whereas *Mankind* is an exemplary dramatisation of one aspect of Mankind's sinfulness, and *Wisdom* a combination of tableau and debate showing selectively the effect of man's behaviour on the soul, and *Everyman* a concentrated teaching of how to face death, *The Castle of Perseverance* attempts to survey the whole of man's life, all aspects of sin, the fate of the soul, the contest between God and the Devil, the need for confession and penitence, and so on, and in order to achieve such a panoramic representation it employs a cast of over 30, is divisible into 23 scenes,[5] some of which are very long, is constructed as an attenuated sequence, and has stage setting more suited to a spectacular *auto da fe* than to a domestic entertainment.

One can see interesting connections and comparisons with *The Castle of Perseverance* in several different directions. First, one can compare the play with other treatments of the themes, particularly that of the Ages of Man. Secondly, one can compare it with other large-scale plays. Thirdly, one can see it as an allegorical parallel to the scriptural cycles.

2. *'All human life is here!'*

Long educational works, both secular and religious, are a characteristic product of the Middle Ages. Most of the English examples are translations from Latin or French and, if not translations, they are imitations or adaptations of the works of learning which were thought authoritative and valuable. The impulse towards comprehensiveness is thus inherited by Middle English writers from the scholars and churchmen of earlier ages, such as Isidore of Seville, whose early seventh-century *Etymologiae* was one of the influential encyclopaedias of the knowledge of the age and who, like Boethius a hundred years earlier, was one of the Latin writers who passed on the remnants of classical knowledge to the later Middle Ages. One of the signs in fourteenth-century England of the growing acceptance and importance of English as the language of literature, knowledge and culture is the appearance of translations of Latin and French educational works, such as Chaucer's translations of Boethius and the astronomical treatise on *The Astrolabe*. John of Trevisa translated Higden's *Polychronicon*, an exhaustive universal history of the world from

Creation to the fourteenth century, which also covers geography and science, and *De Proprietatibus Rerum*, a huge encyclopaedia of natural science compiled in the thirteenth century by Bartholomaeus Anglicus, drawing on Isidore; this shows the greater boldness of the medieval encyclopaedist in comparison to the modern scientist, since it begins with the nature of God, angels (good and bad) and the soul, before passing to the more corporeal matters of human physiology and disease and the world of plants, animals and birds.[6]

In such works the authors usually tackled a huge area of subject-matter; they surveyed all known history, the complete span of human knowledge, the whole of man's life, all the phenomena of the universe, and so on. The actual knowledge displayed is often partial, confused, mistaken or unreliable, but the authors were doing their best to convey the authoritative views of the writers of the past as fully as they could. This same comprehensiveness of intention passed into poetic narratives and other forms of fiction and in many medieval works factual matter is put into fictional mouths. Even more significant for the study of imaginative literature is the way in which poets accepted and made use of the classifications of history, life and knowledge which were established by the encyclopaedic teachers. In the *Polychronicon*, for instance, one can find the basis of the structural sequence of many literary works in the common division of history into the Seven Ages of the World, an idea going back to the chronicle of Orosius and to his master Augustine, and beyond them to the succession of empires in Daniel's interpretation of Nebuchadnezzar's dream. *De Proprietatibus Rerum* shows us the medieval ways of classifying the facets of life and here we meet the related pattern of the Seven Ages of Man; in this version these proceed from *infancia*, the first childhood, which is 'ful tendre and neische, quabby and gleymy', through *puericia* (7–14), *adholescencia* (14–21, or later in the opinion of some), *juventus* (the age of strength, lasting until 45 or 50), *senecta* (middle age or 'first elde', in which men draw away from youth), *senectus* (the 'secounde elde' lasting until 70), to *senium* (the 'last age' of 'passyng and failyng of wittes'). The relationship of such compendia of knowledge to the comments on human life from medieval preachers, poets and dramatists is occasionally even more strikingly close, when the factual survey suddenly bursts out into reflection and moralisation, as Trevisa, following Bartholomew, following Isidore, suddenly does on the theme of the advantages and disadvantages of age. On the one hand it is:

> Good for it delyvereth us out of the power of myghti men and tirauntis and maketh ende of lust, and breketh of fleischelich likinge, and hath wit and wisdom, and yeveth good counseile as mony olde men don. It is ende of wrecchidnes and of woo, and bigynnynge of welthe of joye, and passinge out of perile and comynge in prise, parfitnes in medeful dedis, and disposicoun to be parfite.[7]

But, on the other hand, it brings 'febilnes and noye' with sickness and failure of natural warmth:

> . . . myght and strengthe passith and failith, fleisch and fairnes is consumpt and spendith, the skyn rivelith, the sinewis schrinken, the body bendith and croketh, fourme and schap is ilost, fairnes of the body brought to nought. Alle this failith in elde. Alle men dispisen the olde man and ben hevy and wery of him. The olde man is itraveiled and greved with coughynge and spettynge and with other greves, forto asschen tofalle and turne in asschen, and poudre into poudre. By this space and passing of tyme and of age philosophris discriven mannes lif, in the whiche passing of tyme and of age man chaunchith and drawith alwey toward his ende and to the yatis of deeth.[8]

The Ages of Man is only one of the comprehensive classifications that one meets in the even more specifically moralistic works of medieval Christian teachers writing for the laity about conduct and belief rather than history and science and it is, I hope, unnecessary to cite dozens of exhaustive surveys of sin, collections of sermons for every Sunday in the year, collections of saints' lives, and manuals of instruction to prove the tendency towards comprehensive, encyclopaedic coverage in medieval morality, doctrine and hagiography.

The whole life of man was the subject of constant scrutiny and analysis, and in *The Castle of Perseverance* there are many resemblances and echoes.[9] It was particularly in long vision-poems and allegorical narratives that the themes of the stages of man's life on earth, the conflict between vices and virtues and the figurative castle were elaborated in fourteenth-century and fifteenth-century writing. Again the subject is far too large for a full exploration but a few examples will illustrate the traditions upon which *The Castle of Perseverance* draws.

One detailed fourteenth-century poetic and comprehensive view of man and the world is found in Gower's *Mirour de l'Omme*, his long allegorical poem in French. Here Gower dealt with the genealogy of the sins, tracing the birth of the Seven Deadly Sins from the union of Death and Sin (children of the Devil) and the subsequent birth of five children to each Sin from union with the World. Fortunately Reason is equally philoprogenitive and the Seven Virtues equally fecund. So we have a comprehensive classification of sin and virtue and their sub-types, and these 70 pigeon-holes can then be used to file away the examples of corruption that Gower finds in the various estates of society. In his Latin poem about the sad state of affairs in contemporary England, *Vox Clamantis*, Gower pictures the sins at work in man as microcosm and the whole social order as macrocosm, and in his English poem *Confessio Amantis* he not only applies the full range of sins and their sub-types to the subject of love, but also summarizes history in terms of the succession of the Ages and Empires of the World.[10]

That other voluminous medieval poet, Lydgate, contributed hugely to the comprehensive coverage of history, man's life, religion, practical knowledge and much else. His version of *The Pilgrimage of the Life of Man*, translated from the French of Deguileville, brings into English an influential, if dreary, moral allegory of the journey of man's life, which has a figurative castle (the house of Grace-Dieu where the dreamer in this vision-poem is instructed before setting out on the pilgrimage), a pilgrim's progress with encounters with various sins, another castle, the coming of Age and the preparation for Death. In *The Court of Sapience*, an anonymous poem once attributed to Lydgate but more clearly and elegantly written than he was capable of, is a scholarly, rhetorical version of the debate of the daughters of God, followed by a second book in which there is an allegorical journey, a figurative castle (the court of Sapience) and an encyclopaedic catalogue of the features of the natural world and of the main subjects of medieval academic study.[11] In the early sixteenth century this current of literary history follows on through Stephen Hawes's *The Pastime of Pleasure*, a huge allegorical journey for the hero, Graunde Amoure, through the Active Life, knowledge, chivalry, war, love and chastity to marriage with La Bel Pucell, but subsequent decline as Old Age approaches into avarice, from which he is rescued in the nick of time by Contrition and Conscience.[12] Beyond this lies *The Faerie Queene*: Spenser transforms the material into something new but the long tradition of medieval moral allegory, of journeys, battles and castles, of large-scale panoramas of figures, scenes and pictures, is clearly recognisable.

The length and inclusiveness of *The Castle of Perseverance* is a reflection of the sort of love of classification and of thoroughness which these literary traditions exemplify. Compared to some long narrative works, the play is, in fact, selective. There is a complete cast of sins and virtues, but the progress of man from the cradle to the grave is presented as beginning, middle and end rather than pursued through all its possible stages. This is true, of course, of other treatments of the Ages of Man, and often these are more memorable than the full versions – the version of Youth which Chaucer turned into the Squire, for instance, or which became the figure of Hick Scorner, or the version of Elde in *The Pardoner's Tale*. The fourteenth-century alliterative poem *The Parliament of the Three Ages* presents a vivid, fairly economical picture of Youth, Middle Age and Old Age, in their characteristic garbs, occupations and habits of mind; here it is Middle Age who is preoccupied with money and possessions, while Old Age's thoughts are of mortality.[13] The other method of selection is to use a large number of classifications, but to illustrate each one briefly. The poem 'The Mirror of the Periods of Man's Life', written at about the same time as *The Castle of Perseverance*, is an instance.[14] In 656 lines (in 8-line stanzas) the poet deals with the outline of the material of *The Castle of Perseverance* and of *The Pilgrimage of the Life of Man* and of many another fifteenth-century moral work. The new-born child sets off into the wilderness, accompanied by a good and an evil angel, on the fearful pilgrimage to seek death, in order to separate the soul from the body. The poet jumps from age to age, from infancy to 7, then to 14 and to 20, where the Seven Virtues and the Seven Mortal Sins contend for him, he rejects Conscience in favour of Freewill and listens to the teaching of the Sins; at 30 he boasts, at 40 and 50 he is dominated by Covetousness and ignores the warnings of Conscience; at 60 he begins to repent and to regret his wasted life and to feel the threat of Death:

> Feendis threten faste to take me,
> And steeren helle houndis to bite me;
> Deeth seith my breed he hath baken me;
> Now schaketh he his spere to smite me.
> Thus I am huntid as an herte to abay,
> I not whidir Y may me turne . . .
> To flee to God is my beste way,
> There schal Y in no poynt spurne.   (397 . . . 406)

The poem ends in lengthy expression of the regrets of age, and in this emphasis it identifies itself with the tradition of mortality lyrics spoken by old men (e.g. 'An Old Man's Prayer' in the Harley collection), but the machinery of the sins and virtues continues through to the end with the alternate voices of Man and the personified moral qualities expressing the stages of learning to die. The voice of the poet takes over to offer the poem to us as a mirror in which we may see ourselves reflected. Much of the poem is in direct speech, as are many moral lyrics of the fifteenth century, and the dramatic effect of the spoken word gives it its life and makes it suitable for adaptation into stage drama. It is, in fact, a possible source for the version of the Ages of Man which makes the most interesting comparison with *The Castle of Perseverance*, the early sixteenth-century play *Mundus et Infans*.[15]

The theme of this drama is no surprise: again we meet the course of man's life from cradle to grave and the conflict between good and evil for man's soul. The interest is in the way that in this version the subject has been fined down to a series of dialogues which could be played by two, or at most three, actors.[16] The beginning is dominated by Mundus, the World, who boasts of his palace, his riches and plenty, and controls the stages of man's life by supplying him both with a succession of names and with opportunities to grow in the ways of worldly pleasure. So the Child is clothed, named Wanton and encouraged to games and pranks, re-named Love, Lust and Liking and turned to lewdness and vanity, renamed Manhood and given fine clothing, lands and rents, dubbed a knight and encouraged (after learning of the seven kings who serve the World) to seek adventure, conquest and lordly pride, and to boast of power. The beginning of the play thus traces the triumph of the World and then Mundus departs, since Manhood himself has achieved the qualities of the World and takes over the role of boastful vainglory. The entry of Conscience begins the second stage, in which Manhood at first

118

rejects with scorn the warnings of Conscience, but is gradually prised from the sins in turn by the lesson of moderation:

Manhood　What! Conscyence, shold I leve all game and gle?

Conscience　Nay, Manhode, so mote I thye,
　　　　　　All myrthe in mesure is good for the,
　　　　　　But, syr, measure is in all thynge.　(449–52)

But, though he accepts Conscience's teaching, Manhood is not able yet to reject the World ('For mankynde he doth mery make'). Conscience is succeeded by Folly, in whom all seven sins are subsumed, who rejects Conscience in no uncertain terms:

　　　　　A cuckoo for Conscyence! he is but a dawe!
　　　　　He can not elles but preche.　(625–6)

Folly is a typical Vice figure. He speaks confidential asides to the audience, talks much vapid levity about taverns, fighting and lechery, lures Manhood to Eastcheap and mockingly gives Manhood a new name, Shame. The third and final stage of the play begins with Conscience's moralising comments on the

　　　　　　　　. . . freylnes of Mankynde,
　　　　How oft he falleth in folye,
　　　　Through temptacyon of the fende;
　　　　For whan the fende and the flesshe be at one assent,
　　　　Than Conscyence clere is clene out-cast.　(722–6)

Perseverance takes over from Conscience and confronts Manhood, now transformed into Age and complaining of loss of pleasure, strength and possession; his repentance centres on the name of Shame given him by Folly, and Perseverance teaches him the way to salvation with a new name with which to face death, Repentance.

So one can recognise in the play the three stages of *The Castle of Perseverance*, the taking-on of the World, the impulse towards virtue checked by a conflict between Virtue and Vice which the latter wins, and the final scenes of age and regret. But in *Mundus et Infans* the enactment of the stages is in skeleton outline, with Conscience and Folly representing the range of virtue and vice in the centre of the play. It is focused on two related features: first the series of encounters between man and another figure, whereby the World is replaced in turn by Conscience, Folly, Conscience again and Perseverance (the pattern which Milton used in *Samson Agonistes*); and secondly the suggestive and effective fluidity in man's nature which is conveyed by the succession of names, which indicate not only the tradition of the Ages of Man, but also identify the development of his moral state.

The comparison with *The Castle of Perseverance* is revealing of the qualities of both. The central figure of *Mundus et Infans* is (despite his changes of name and personality) an interesting core to the play, whereas Humanum Genus is not. The limited number of figures concentrates the audience's mind on simple, clearly focused examples of contrary persuasions to folly and to strength of purpose. By contrast *The Castle of Perseverance* belongs with the grand, encyclopaedic intentions of early fifteenth-century translators, moralists and narrative poets. The themes are very similar to those used by the later playwright, but here is the full-scale version, with all the sins, all the virtues, good and bad angels, God and the Devil, the World and the Flesh, presented in a grandiose stage setting which represents all the corners of the earth, and beyond. While the author of *Mundus et Infans* shows how one could represent on stage the whole of human life in a few sketched moments, *The Castle of Perseverance* tries to represent it all more completely and impressively: the conflict between good and evil is, as a result, far more powerful, but the wood of Mankind's life-history gets lost in the trees. The contrast between the two is a fundamental difference between drama moving in the direction of the symbolic moment which encapsulates life (the Beckett path) and drama moving in the direction of lengthy coverage, often repetitious and tedious, but eventually massive and cumulatively powerful (the O'Neill way).

3. *Medley, Panorama and Chronicle*

There are three single plays surviving from before 1525 which have a scale and scope comparable to those of *The Castle of Perseverance*: *Mary Magdalene*, Henry Medwall's *Nature* and John Skelton's *Magnificence*. The first is an interesting medley and deserves to be better known; the others I will look at more briefly.

The late fifteenth- or early sixteenth-century plays known as the Digby Plays have never been prominent in discussions of medieval English drama, partly because they do not fit neatly into the pigeon-holes labelled 'morality play', 'mystery play', etc. The most varied of them, *Mary Magdalene*, is described by Rosemary Woolf as 'a hybrid curiosity, part mystery play, part saint's life, part morality play with realistic low-life elements'.[17] If one were being more unkind, one would call it a hotch-potch, but it has considerable interest for the student of medieval drama, nevertheless.

Embedded within the series of incidents from the life of Mary Magdalene, whose Biblical identity is fused with that of Mary, the sister of

Lazarus, is a self-contained group of allegorical scenes which follow the pattern of temptation, sin and repentance which some would consider as a major defining characteristic of the morality play. This group begins, after the scene of the death of Cyrus, Mary's father, with a set of speeches from the World, the Flesh and the Devil and their supporters. The King of the World boasts of his power over men through his control of the wheel of Fortune and of the seven metals, which are linked to the seven planets and their influence over men and are also the sources of the wealth of the seven princes of Hell. Pride and Covetousness declare themselves his supporters. Then the King of the Flesh, supported by Sloth, Gluttony and Lechery, boasts of his power over delights and pleasures, symbolised by flowers and herbs. Satan enters 'in a stage' with Hell beneath, with Wrath and Envy as his retainers, boasting of his power to use snares:

> Mannis sowle to besegyn and bryng to obeysauns.   (364)

Once the ritual declarations of nature and intent are complete, Satan consults the World who sends his messenger, Sensuality, for Flesh; the three confer about the virtuous Mary, of whom it is said:

> If she in vertu stylle may dwelle,
> She xal byn abyll to dystroye helle.   (419–20)

Lechery and the Bad Angel are in turn summoned to aid in the temptation and seduction of the Magdalene, and the stage direction indicates that we are then to envisage the Castle of Maudleyn besieged by the Sins and entered by Lechery (and the Bad Angel) who flatters Mary's beauty with a flourish of aureate language:

> Heyl, lady most laudabyll of alyauns!
> Heyl, oryent, as the sonne in his reflexite!   (440–1)

Whether or not this is intended as a parody of aureate lyrics addressed to the Virgin, it shows an association between aureation and insincerity, which is more immediately (perhaps more superficially) effective than the use of the exaggerated style to indicate majesty or sanctity. Mary's reply shows, by style as well as content, that she is susceptible to such specious praise:

> Your debonarius obedyauns ravyssyt me to trankquilyte!   (447)

In no time we are taken off to a tavern in Jerusalem where a boasting taverner plies Mary with drink and she is presented with a lover, a gallant (identified as Curiosity, a Dandy) who has the usual speech identifying his nature – here an enthusiasm for women, love and elegance. The conversation between Mary and the Dandy is the first extended dialogue in the play (the scenes are mainly short and scrappy, consisting of opening boast, short follow-up to advance the business and then a scene-change) and the result is a comic little love-scene, which consists in part of a pastiche of the courtly love-lyric:

> A! dere dewchesse, my deysyys Iee
> Splendaunt of colour, most of femynyte,
> Your sofreyn colours set with synseryte!
> Conseder my love into yower alye,
> Or elles I am smet with peynnes of perplexite!   (515–9)

This particular bubble of pretentiousness is pricked by Mary, despite her susceptibility, with a tart answer:

> Why, sir, wene ye that I were a kelle? (*whore*)   (520)

which perhaps shows that the dramatist is more concerned with the effect of the moment than with over-all consistency of tone and character. Satan, the World and the Flesh briefly glory in Mary's seduction and an elaborate stage direction (despatching Satan 'hom to his stage', placing the seven sins dressed as devils in waiting in the house of Simon the leper and Mary in 'an erbyr') prepares for the repentance scene. With as little psychological realism as in the earlier seduction, the dramatist presents Mary's return to virtue through the reproof of the Good Angel:

> Woman, woman, why art thou so on-stabyll?   (588)

Mary seeks Jesus, finds him in Simon's house, washes his feet with her tears and dries them with her hair, expresses her penitence, is forgiven by Jesus, at which the seven devils depart from her. Before leaving the theme and returning to the Biblical material of the death of Lazarus, the playwright adds an epilogue of grotesque comedy in which Satan expresses his fury at the defeat of his plans, and has the Bad Angel and the seven devils who were the Deadly Sins all beaten on the buttocks as a punishment for their poor efforts; the scene ends in smoke and soot as the devils set a house on fire and they all sink to Hell.

These scenes convey no great moral force, largely because they are short and the ideas of sin, guilt and repentance are so perfunctorily presented, but they are lively enough in their way, and suggest that the theme of temptation of virtue, its fall into sin and subsequent recovery was a conventional dramatic motif with which a play could be diversified, and that the theme was automatically seen in terms of a plot of devils and vices against the innocent human figure, whether or not the play otherwise made use of personification of moral ideas.

The scenes which precede and follow this allegory are in the manner of Scriptural pageant, except that a large number of figures appears, not all of them necessary to the main story of Martha, Mary and the death and raising of their brother. The appearance and disappearance in turn, at the beginning of the play, of Tiberius, Herod and Pilate, all with ranting, boasting speeches, gives to the play a haphazard quality, as if the characters are plucked from the air and discarded, and this makes the intrusion of the personifications less startling than it otherwise would have been. The same is true after the raising of Lazarus (the end of Part I of the play), when yet another king, the King of Marseilles (representing all heathendom), appears with rant and excessive uxoriousness, followed by his effusive wife, and initiates a new phase of the drama in which devout scenes of the three Maries at the tomb appear between a devil bellowing and roaring his distress at the Harrowing of Hell, and a heathen priest and his boy engaging in farcical knock-about, scurrilous banter and a mock-Latin service. The latter part of the play concentrates on Mary Magdalene's fulfilment of Christ's command to go as apostle to Marseilles. This is dramatised spectacularly by means of a moving ship brought into the acting area, first for Mary's journey to Marseilles, then for the King and Queen's penitent journey to the Holy Land (during which there is a violent storm, the Queen gives birth and dies, and mother and child are left on a rock), and for a third time when the King returns to Marseilles (finding wife and son miraculously alive on the rock through the Magdalene's aid). In addition Mary's conversion of the King and Queen is effected by the setting on fire of the heathen temple and the sinking of the priest to Hell, and the play ends with further transformations and machines as angels appear in the clouds and draw Mary up from the wilderness to feed her, and as Mary's death-scene shows simultaneous actions on earth and in heaven.

The latter part of the play thus turns away from allegorical action into a mixture of comedy, sanctity and the exploitation of the physical possibilities of a fixed place-and-scaffold staging to suggest the wondrous, romantic nature of the journeys and miracles typical of the saint's life. The total effect is of a sort of pantomime, lively both in comedy and the spectacular, but neither discriminating nor consistent in its use of any of its effects and tones. I suggest that there are two interesting conclusions to be drawn.

First, the nature of *Mary Magdalene* is surely the result of some kind of dramatic process which may fairly be called popularisation. The morality plays themselves have often been called the 'popular drama' of the late medieval period, because of their use of comedy, their possible association with professional companies of travelling players, the local references, and so on, but some of the moral plays possess features which suggest both a scholarly playwright and a sophisticated audience. In *Mary Magdalene* there are several characteristics which suggest a 'popular', not very sophisticated writer, audience and intention. There is, for one, the extent of the dramatist's reliance on conventional dramatic devices. He obviously reckons that to open with a speech of ranting boast by a powerful ruler is a surefire success with an audience. The beginning of the play has a series of them, for Tiberius (1–19), Herod (140–66), Pilate

(229–43) and the King of the World (305–25), and the King of Marseilles kicks off the second half of the play in the same style:

> Avantt, avant the, onworthy wrecchesse!
> Why lowtt ye nat low to my lawdabyll presens,
> Ye brawlyng breelles, and blabyr-lyppyd bycchys,
> Obedyenly to obbey me withowt offense?   (925–8)

Many other speeches belong to familiar types: many of the speeches given to Mary (and to Martha and Lazarus) are essentially exclamatory expressions – of praise, repentance, subjection, sorrow – with no development within themselves or any relationship with the speech of others; they open with 'A' or 'O' or 'Alas!', indicate the emotion and then amplify it. Again the dramatist makes heavy use of catch-phrases as means of identifying figures and types. If kings boast, devils roar:

> A, owt, owt and harrow! I am hampered with hate   (722)

yells Satan as Mary repents and is echoed by his fellow demon when Christ harrows Hell. Similarly the gallant, Curiosity, has the necessary tag:

> Hof, hof, hof, a frysch new galaunt   (491)

The element of rather crude mockery and parody in the play, such as the boy's mock-service with its gobble-de-gook Latin ('snyguer-snagoer-werwolfforum', etc.) (1186–1201), is used only for a momentary laugh and has no consistent satirical effect or relevance to the play's central subject. The over-all mixture and sense of haphazard lurching from scene to scene and style to style suggests an attempt to manufacture dramatic appeal. This is apparent too in the theatrical showmanship and the exploitation of props: the scenes with the ship give the impression of having been invented to make use of the mechanism rather than the other way round.

The other aspect I find of interest is the sense that the type of play being created is a large-scale compendium of dramatic themes and effects. It is a panoramic play with a lot of different settings, a long list of characters, a large span of time, a mixture of ideas, several different stages in the plot – or rather several plots. It is as if the playwright wanted to get as much in as he could, as many moods and themes as could be hung on the central figure. The play as a whole becomes a loose, baggy chronicle.

Though *Mary Magdalene* is a hybrid, and not a well-written play, it has enough features in common with the other long plays I mentioned to support the idea of the large-scale, panoramic play as a dramatic type. The idea could have originated in the Corpus Christi Cycle itself, which is one play in a long series of scenes, and which could be presented (and probably was in the case of the N-Town cycle) in one place, and acted (as nowadays) by one cast rather than by separate groups. The survey of the history of man from Creation to Judgment needs a long time and a lot of scenes, even if much is left out. The life of an individual man or woman does not necessarily do so (and so could be presented quite briefly as in *Mundus et Infans*), but it could be treated lengthily, if it was analysed into phases and influences, or if man was shown as part of a varied world and society. This is what has happened in the longer medieval single plays. In *Mary Magdalene* we see one version, possibly a popular or degenerate one, of the panorama of a religious life. *The Castle of Perseverance* is an earlier version which may have influenced later panoramic plays.

A later version, of a less popular cast, was produced for performance in the great hall of a Tudor mansion by Henry Medwall, chaplain to Cardinal John Morton, Archbishop of Canterbury and Lord Chancellor to Henry VII, and manipulator of the famous 'fork' technique of extracting money from rich and poor. Whether the same flexibility of approach was responsible for his chaplain's two surviving contributions to early drama one cannot know, but the secular comic medley of *Fulgens and Lucrece* shows Medwall in a rather different, light-hearted mood, in comparison to the weighty, two-part allegorical play *Nature* (c.1495).[18] Medwall here sets himself to treat the familiar theme of the contest for influence over Man between Reason and Sensuality. He begins with an astonishingly long speech for the goddess Nature (lines 1–105) in which she explains the order of the universe and the nature of man. Under Nature's rule Man chooses Reason as his adviser and enters the court of the World; World clothes Man in suitable garb and turns him into a worldly man, whose development is marked by his dismissal of his old nurse, Innocence. In the early scenes the interest is in the quite sophisticated treatment of Man's behaviour: the loss of innocence and growth of worldliness is seen to be a natural development, an inevitable result of engaging in any social activity. The figure of Man is a more equivocal character than in the earlier allegorical plays, more like a natural man than an abstraction. The play still turns on his moral choices and the exercise of free will, but the choices are seen as complicated. The first half of the play is completed by the course of descent into sin and the recoiling movement towards repentance. Sensuality becomes the powerful influence, engaging Pride as Man's servant and bringing about scenes of corruption as Pride's six kinsmen enter Man's service under assumed names. The impulse to repentance is achieved through Reason and Shamefacedness, and the first part ends with Man asking Reason for help in acknowledging his wrongdoing.

The pattern of innocence, sin and repentance is repeated in the second half of the play with variations. After a sermon from Reason on the evils of the World, Flesh and Devil, Sensuality returns and Man is soon won back to sin. The play reverts to Medwall's main interest, satirical pictures of a sinful household, with the Deadly Sins in turn demonstrating their tastes: Pride orders new clothes, Wrath quarrels and Lechery exerts her pull on

Man through his return to his whore Margery (who has entered a nunnery and become Sister Margery but who is no more steadfast in faith than Man himself). In these scenes the quality of the writing moves towards a sort of comic realism in that the life of the audience for which the play was written is reflected in the nature of the setting and action. This is a play for a great household which shows the audience a grotesque picture of itself; there is an element of localisation in the allegory which no doubt gave a mocking bite to the play which is difficult for the modern reader to catch. Man becomes the head of a house and the other figures retainers, courtiers and servants. The play is thus more in contact with experience of the world than some allegorical drama, but it ends in conventional religious vein as, with the coming of Age, Man is led back to the figure of Reason by an unusually long list of those allegorical social workers necessary to the process of repentance – Meekness, Charity, Patience, Good Occupation, Liberality, Abstinence and Chastity as the contraries of the Deadly Sins.

Medwall's *Nature* shows how the themes of the moral plays were to broaden out into the treatment of social life with a more secular emphasis: one could argue that the same process involved a narrowing as much as a broadening, of course, since the universality of the moral themes is gradually blurred as the figures become individual cases. There is also some attempt on Medwall's part to develop argument in the play, particularly in the debate at the beginning about Nature and Man's role in the world. The play is thus of interest in terms of the historical development of the allegorical drama. With *Magnificence* it shows the continuation of a technique with a change of subject-matter. The perspective becomes worldly, political and social, and even in the stage of repentance, the emphasis is on a return to socially healthy conduct and not just the preparation for death. The plays represent a step on the way to later political and historical drama about order and government, as well as humanist debates about knowledge, the logic of human society and so on. But to imply, because one can see in *Nature* historical significance, that it is a good play or a better play than *The Castle of Perseverance* would be even more false than to attribute achievement to *Fulgens and Lucrece*; in some ways *Nature* represents a regression to the weakest aspects of *The Castle of Perseverance*. If *Mary Magdalene* shows the impulse to create a substantial entertainment resulting in an indiscriminate hotch-potch, what one sees produced by a similar impulse in *Nature* is a laboured instance of long-winded mediocrity.[19] Neither in expression nor in staging is *Nature* capable of gripping an audience. The Digby play illustrates the coarsening effect of popularisation and sensationalism; *Nature* illustrates the dire effects of small talents being encouraged by private patronage.

Skelton had more talent and he wrote for a more talented and more powerful master, but even in his hands the form of the long play is unwieldy and tedious in places. The strength of *Magnificence* is a more interestingly characterised hero, whose function in the world has the individuality of the problems of the Tudor monarchy as well as the universality of the great man's moral choices, and a more effective over-all structure than the earlier two-part pattern of *The Castle of Perseverance*, *Mary Magdalene* and *Nature*. Instead of the duplicating effect of a mid-play defeat of vice and a subsequent relapse into sin (or in the Digby play the introduction of new characters to illustrate the further combatting of evil), Skelton's action describes one arc. The succession of stages of Magnificence's descent from prosperity to degradation and the subsequent moderate rise to a state of Measure is one of the versions of the turn of Fortune's wheel which was associated with literary form in the five-book structure of Boethius' *De Consolatione Philosophiae*. Chaucer used the opposite curve of sorrow, happiness, sorrow as his pattern of tragedy in *Troilus and Criseyde*. Both Chaucer's and Skelton's versions are leading to the five-act structure of later drama. There is then in *Magnificence* a convincing over-all pattern of moral action and development which holds together the lengthy series of scenes and speeches. The 'comprehensive' intention is evident in the combination of a serious moral and political theme with the satirical picture of court life projected through the vices and the scenes of intrigue, but there is no attempt, as there is in *Nature*, to express the complete nature of man's life on earth and the organisation of the universe. *Magnificence* is long, spans a large period of time, has a large number of characters and concerns itself with significant issues, but, in comparison with *Nature* and *The Castle of Perseverance*, it is more concentrated and better focused on a particular set of ideas. It is not a great play, but it is a coherent and inventive one.

But when all is said and done the only medieval playwrights who handled the form of the long play successfully are the authors of the Scriptural cycles. These are the only plays of the period which remain capable of rousing more than temporary enthusiasm in producers, actors and audience, and the main reason is the obvious one that the life and death of Christ is a gripping and significant narrative. Beyond that is the framework in which the story of Christ is placed, which turns the outline of familiar Old and New Testament history into the easily assimilated and often powerful form of single pageants, tableaux and dialogue. The whole human history is surveyed in outline, from origin to end, but it is presented as an unfolding chronicle, in small units of particular times and places. The sequence is long, but the coverage of the ages of history and the ages of mankind is selective and spare enough for one to see the patterns forming. The basic pattern of Fall, Redemption and Judgment is enriched by the patterns of correspondence, the forecasts of the future and the echoes of the past, the symbolic prefigurings of the role of Christ, the fulfilment of the pre-known destiny. The most convincing reasons justify the length of the cycles: the panorama is a necessary part of the purpose and meaning of the work, existing as a sequence of the historical past and the destined future; the span is logically relevant to the theme of the fulfilment of the Christian scheme.

The main component of the cycles is chronicle in speech form. The dramatists write dialogue when they can, but use explanatory, narrating and identifying long speeches freely. The succession of short units in this form would be (and in places is) very monotonous and limited, but the historical pattern and the epic theme and the epic figure of Christ concentrate the thrust forward of the sequence, grip the imagination, and make the cycle capable, despite verbal and dramatic weaknesses, of moving the audience and carrying one over some flaccid didactic portions to the stirring episodes of the Harrowing of Hell and the Last Judgment.

There is no reason why the allegorical dramatisation of the course of the life of an individual man from birth to death should not have had as powerful a large-scale dramatic treatment. The idea of allegorical treatment of man's life and death has gone on tempting playwrights, but modern versions such as *The Skin of Our Teeth* and *Johnson over Jordan* have not made all that much advance on *The Castle of Perseverance*. Comparison between *The Castle of Perseverance* and the medieval cycles reveals both similarity and differences which go some way to explaining why this particular version can be counted only a partial success.

The similarity is in the sense of which I spoke in the opening chapter that the cycles and the allegorical moral plays are alternative ways of dealing with the same subject-matter, the working-out over a span of time of the Christian scheme of Fall, Redemption and Judgment. In *The Castle of Perseverance* the phase of Creation and Fall is dramatised in the birth of Mankind, the plot of the World, Flesh and Devil against him and his falling into the sinful ways of the world. The phase of Redemption is centred on the allegorical Castle and man's frailty; man's opportunity for virtue and salvation and the conflict between good and evil take the place of the narrative of the life of Christ, and the battle scene provides the epic spectacle parallel to the Passion sequence in the cycles. The phase of Judgment is expressed in the motif of the debate of the Daughters of God and the final voice of the Almighty seated on the throne. So the Christian history is re-enacted in the life of the individual.

The differences between *The Castle of Perseverance* and the cycles, however, put the moral play into perspective. It is clear from the comparison that one of the reasons for the greater effectiveness of the cycles is the variety within them. As the variety and the flexibility of style in *The Canterbury Tales* reveal the limitations of Gower's parallel gathering together of a multitude of stories in *Confessio Amantis*, so with the plays. The changes of style, and indeed the very inconsistencies of treatment, manner and standard prove more appealing than the dogged consistency through a long work of one voice. Chaucer speaks in many voices; Gower has his virtues but range of poetic expression is not one. In the plays it is not one skilled writer that produces the effect, but the accidental mixture that comes from the work of different writers and different periods. The 'composition' of the cycles is one aspect of their meaning. The contrasts and inconsistencies set off questions and comparisons, associations and alternatives in the reader's mind. Hence the least effective of the four more or less complete surviving versions of the Corpus Christi Cycle is that from Chester, which is the most uniform in versification and style. It probably (despite the late date of the text) preserves the greatest degree of the original impulse behind the development of the cycle as a dramatic form. One can see the positive advantages in consistency of tone; it is, specifically, less meretricious than the Wakefield Master is capable of being. But, on the other hand, it is the Cycle least capable of surprising the reader. Both the Towneley Cycle and the N-Town cycle do contain surprises and are the outstanding examples of the good quality fifteenth-century hotch-potch (compared to the poor quality hotch-potch of the *Play of the Sacrament* and the slightly better variety in *Mary Magdalene*). Here one is conscious even in reading, more so in performance, of the quality of a living and developing tradition; both are moving in places, funny in others, satirical and reverent, clumsy and rich. In both, the idea of the cycle just about holds together the pieces, but part of the pleasure and strength of both works is the sense of a loose assemblage of disparate parts held together by an over-riding purpose. Even the York Cycle has some of the weaknesses of the ramshackling together of pieces and has its longueurs and its tracts of flat, lifeless plodding verse, but it gets further than any of the other three in triumphing over the difficulties of the panoramic form. By a combination (resulting from the compilation of the cycle over a period of time and by a variety of writers) of pageants which depend on rhetorical alliterative poetry, pageants which develop the analysis of individual motive and psychology, pageants which depend on symbolic action and a fine series which present the Trials of Jesus and the Crucifixion as the dramatic climax, the York Cycle comes over both as a clear pattern of the working-out of justice through history and as a kaleidoscope of dramatic pieces which take the eye in a variety of ways but remain within their geometrical shape.

CHAPTER SIX

Scope and Style: Lydgate and East Anglian Drama

The point from which I began was the inadequacy of the division of fourteenth- and fifteenth-century plays into the two main classes of scriptural cycles and allegorical morality plays (with a few left-overs identified as saint's plays, etc.). The four earliest 'morality plays', *The Pride of Life* and the three Macro plays, differ from one another, and among them connect with a range of literary ideas and forms, and overlap with non-allegorical plays in important areas of subject-matter and treatment. The variety within the drama is parallel to the variety within medieval English poetry: distinctions of genre are determined by scope and scale as well as by subject-matter and rhetorical devices. Take two fourteenth-century religious narrative poems, *Purity* and *Piers Plowman*, as an example. They have in common alliterative verse, Biblical material, seriousness of intent and poetic skill which can create effects both dramatic and nobly religious. They are usually considered as two separate types of poem because one is allegorical and the other not, but, in truth, the main point of separation is their different scope and structure; the sequential structure of *Purity*, a series of Scriptural narratives somewhat uneasily linked together by passages of didacticism, is so much simpler than the dream-structure of *Piers Plowman*, which keeps returning to the same symbolic figures and representations of humanity, and so creates a cumulative richness of meaning. Of course, one can use the two poems as starting-points for consideration of the differences between historical narrative, where the poet's function is to interpret known figures and events, and dream-poetry, where the poet is freer to explore his own imagination and to envisage figures and actions which embody psychological and moral activity within human nature. The differences between Scriptural and allegorical drama are similar: in Scriptural plays the main actions and figures are fixed by history and tradition whereas the playwright is freer to invent in allegorical plays and has more choices and a greater variety of them. But this distinction identifies a general feature of religious writing of the period, not a feature peculiar to drama.

In the past the main way of pinpointing the features peculiar to drama has been to focus on the evidence of performance, and to consider plays in terms of the kind of theatre and audience for which they were designed, questions of the history of the development of liturgical into civic production, of processional and static staging, of wagons and arenas, costumes and props, amateur and professional actors. There is still much to be discovered about the circumstances in which plays came into being.

Recent work has emphasised the production of plays in great house-holds, university drama, the particular political and social conditions which explain references within plays, their stylistic features and their scale and range.[1] I believe that exploration of dramatic kinds also has much to tell about audiences, tastes, literary ideas and the other aspects of the history of drama. The traditional dramatic divisions into tragedy, comedy, history and such sub-types as masque are at least as useful for medieval plays as they are for later drama, and the use of these accepted terms serves the plays better than the tendency of 'morality play' etc. to isolate medieval drama into special archaic categories. Also to consider plays as attempts at or versions of tragedy, comedy and the rest focuses attention on their effectiveness and interest as plays much more than classification in terms of subject-matter, or technique, or theatrical and social history.

The medieval plays may be seen as significantly different from one another once one stops approaching them with the pre-judgments implied by identifying them too simply. They are varied both in themselves and in the potential one can see within them with the hindsight knowledge of Elizabethan and Jacobean drama. Such richness as they have is perhaps most engaging in this sense of potential; there are no fifteenth-century dramatic masterpieces, and partial successes (or worse) invite damning comment on their weakest features. But even within only partly effective works one ought to be able to recognise the exploration and the growing diversity of the dramatic medium.

This diversity was the result of several areas of growth in the late medieval period in England. First, medieval plays drew on the variety and quantity of English poetry from the late fourteenth century on; Chaucer, Langland, the *Gawain*-Poet and Gower explored Scriptural narrative, allegorical dream-poetry, morality and satire, romance and realism, as well as establishing a variety of poetic styles suitable for the expression of serious and comic themes. Fifteenth-century poets imitated them, particularly Chaucer, and found their own ways (not necessarily successful) of elaborating on their predecessors' ideas.

Secondly, the fifteenth century saw a very large number of translations into English of literary and educational, non-literary works in verse and prose from Latin, French and other European languages, and, in common with other writers, the dramatists drew in various ways from this new reservoir of material.

Thirdly, the development of private theatres in great houses and of small groups of actors to perform in them, and the existence of groups of travelling actors both encouraged the creation of more new plays and of new types of play. The travelling actors particularly were likely to have encouraged the incorporation of features of popular drama into literary plays. This may be observed, for instance, in Medwall's use in *Fulgens and Lucrece* of Christmas games, of songs, wrestling, jousting and physical horse-play. *Mankind* too has been seen as a popular play, 'a culmination of the most popular elements in the late medieval English stage', partly because of features borrowed from folk-drama.[2] It has been visualised, largely because of this popular veneer, as performed in an inn-yard or within an inn by travelling players. But, as Southern has argued, the hall of a great house is perhaps as likely a venue for this play as for Medwall's dramas for the household of Cardinal Morton.[3] The scholarly tone of the more elevated speeches and the pedantic nature of some of the jokes (puns and word-play, mockery not only of Latin but also in Latin) make one question the 'popular' idea. There is much in the play which suggests that it was written by someone with learning, for an audience of like men, who would enjoy jokes at learning's expense and some ribaldry thrown in. In fact it sounds like a comic university play written for, and possibly by, students. Private auspices and a sophisticated audience are implied,[4] and Axton's idea of 'the Shrovetide *jeu d'esprit* of a group of Cambridge clerks' has much to be said for it – the play can readily be seen as Pancake Day fun in an academic version.[5]

The most important single figure in the late medieval period in the translation, adaptation and popularisation in the English tongue of material first treated in other languages was Lydgate, indefatigable monk and socialite, author of epic and lyric, prayer and satire, fable and tragedy, a sort of Liszt of Bury St Edmunds: his influence on drama is not confined to his composition of Mummings. The importance of East Anglia in the history of medieval drama is partly due to him and the frequent occurrence of the name of Bury St Edmunds in the history of medieval plays and their manuscripts results from the fact that it was in the Abbey there that Lydgate spent a good part of his life. The Benedictine Abbey of Bury has a distinguished history quite apart from Lydgate, of course. As a shrine, as a centre of learning, as the origin of some of the finest of medieval English manuscripts, and as the possessor of a very well-stocked library by fifteenth-century standards, it is important to the general history of English culture in the later Middle Ages. As the place where the barons swore to force King John to accept the terms of Magna Carta it had a tradition of involvement in major political affairs and it has many scattered connections with national events and the fortunes of monarchs and nobles: in 1447, for instance, it was in the refectory of the Abbey that Parliament assembled, in the vengeful presence of Queen Margaret, to agree to issue a warrant for the arrest of Humphrey, Duke of Gloucester. In its own history the Abbey displayed some of the favourite themes of medieval moralists; it suffered the vicissitudes of fortune notably in 1465 when much of the Abbey was destroyed by fire, but it rose again from its ashes (so that John Leland, writing in 1538 could describe it as like a city because of its many gates and towers and its stately church), only to suffer again at the Dissolution. It was during Lydgate's time, however, that the Abbey seems to have been particularly important in the development of English writing and this was the result of royal connections and patronage. Henry VI had close relations with William Curteys,

Abbot from 1429 to 1446, and the relationship had been established during a long visit the King had paid to the Abbey, as a boy of 12, from Christmas 1433 to Easter 1434; during this visit Curteys asked Lydgate to write his *Life of St Edmund* and the presentation copy is a particularly rich example of fifteenth-century manuscript illumination. Lydgate had already established himself as a 'laureate' poet by this time and his presence in the Abbey must surely have been one of the reasons for the length of the King's stay. Many of Lydgate's noble patrons were visitors to the Abbey, and, though in Henry VI's case there may have been a greater devoutness than was found in some of the other visitors, it is clear that the King's visit was a social as well as a religious occasion. He was greeted on his arrival with a ceremonial procession, with the monks in their richest array; during the stay the courtiers hunted and engaged in fishing and falconry; the visit culminated in the solemn ceremonies of Holy Week and the admission of the King, together with his brother (Humphrey, Duke of Gloucester, again) and others of the court to the religious privileges of the monks of the Abbey. It seems likely, given Lydgate's record as the creator of ceremonial verse for all occasions, that poetry, pageant, tableau and other forms of literary and dramatic celebration and entertainment were part of the festivities and observances during this long period of the fusion of court and religious house.[6]

Among the laureate compositions which had established Lydgate's claims on royal favour was his devising of a celebratory poem and the accompanying tableaux and scenes to welcome the young King back to London in 1432 on his return from a lack-lustre coronation ceremony in Paris. Lydgate gives his own account of the pageants in his *King Henry VI's Entry into London* (known also as the *Triumphal Entry*),[7] and the series of elaborate allegorical tableaux, presented at seven stations between London Bridge and St Paul's, combine heraldry, morality, poetry and song. The cardinal virtues, the liberal arts, figures from the Old Testament, the Holy Trinity and figures of angels, all appear in a series of decorative displays, full of symbolic properties and settings, such as swords and shields, thrones, the paradisal garden and a fountain flowing with wine. Lydgate's talents for pomp and ostentation were well adapted to this sort of public art and it is in the creation of a style of ceremonial pageant that Lydgate's greatest contribution to fifteenth-century theatre is found. An even more striking instance (to the student of medieval drama, that is) is the ceremony for the Entry of Queen Margaret, performed in London after Henry VI's marriage to Margaret of Anjou in 1445. It is not known if Lydgate here devised or superintended the tableaux, but he wrote the ceremonial verses. The pageants began on London Bridge with a stage, inscribed with a verse from Genesis, bearing Peace and Plenty, and a second pageant, in the middle of the bridge, representing Noah's Ark; Lydgate's verses extol Margaret as the dove with the olive branch, which is about as ironic an indication as one could get of the degree of realism in such dramatic presentations. The other pageants included at least one real 'play', another version of the debate of the Four Daughters of God, performed on a stage in Leadenhall. In Cornhill the legend of St Margaret was depicted, and was followed by a pageant of the wise and foolish virgins and more religious pageants as the procession neared St Paul's represented the bliss of the Promised Land, the Heavenly Jerusalem and, lastly, opposite St Paul's Gate, the Resurrection and Last Judgment. It is in such public, semi-dramatic performances that one finds a significant meeting-place of Scripture, allegory and saint's life, of impressive pictures and official, rather characterless, poetry, of devotion and ostentation, of morality and pomp. Here is one of the melting-pots in which one can see later medieval drama being shaped; the combination of the scope of the Corpus Christi cycle from Genesis to Judgment with the structure of a medley-series of symbolic pictures (in the manner of such plays as *Mary Magdalene*) shows, working together, features of the drama which have too often been treated as separate.

Two other aspects of Lydgate's life and work are significant with regard to the development and range of fifteenth-century literature. First is his connection with the Chaucer family. This probably began with Lydgate making the acquaintance of Thomas Chaucer, son of the poet, when Lydgate was at Oxford and Thomas, as a result of his marriage to an Oxfordshire heiress, established at the manor of Ewelme. Thomas was a man of public position, M.P. for Oxfordshire, Speaker of the House of Commons and member of the Council in 1424–5. He had connections, through Philippa Swynford his mother, with the Beauforts, sons of John of Gaunt's third marriage to Katherine Swynford, Philippa's sister, regents during Henry VI's minority. Lydgate not only wrote poems for the Chaucer household, but through Thomas made important contacts, with Humphrey, Duke of Gloucester, probably, with the Earl of Warwick, and particularly with the second and third husbands of Alice Chaucer, Thomas's only child. Her second husband was the Earl of Salisbury, who commissioned Lydgate's *Pilgrimage of the Life of Man* in 1426, and her third was William de la Pole, Earl of Suffolk. For Alice herself Lydgate wrote *The Virtues of the Mass* and Suffolk, who was a great landowner in East Anglia and had close connections with the Abbey of Bury St Edmunds, was a poet, a patron of poets and gaoler, friend and possible translator of the sophisticated French aristocratic poet Charles, Duke of Orleans. Suffolk was to the fore in the arrangements for the marriage of Henry VI and Margaret of Anjou and it could have been he who invited Lydgate to have a hand in the street-pageants at *Queen Margaret's Entry into London*.[8] Through the Chaucer connection Lydgate found many opportunities for and stimuli to the creation of courtly works of various kinds; probably among them were examples of the verses for tableaux and the creation of semi-dramatic public, ceremonial displays, such as may be seen in the Mummings and Entries. The connection also kept up Lydgate's association with Oxford, so that in him there is a significant cultural bridge between Oxford and Cambridge. And it was from the patronage of the great abbeys, the great houses and the universities in the fifteenth century that ceremonies and entertainments grew into the various types of drama which have been described in earlier chapters.

The second significant feature in Lydgate's work was the result of his writing for aristocratic patrons: his development of an inflated, elevated poetic style. His works were so often of a public, formal kind that he fell into the mannerisms of platform rhetoric, amplificatory, sententious, Latinate and embellished. It is from Lydgate that contemporary and later fifteenth-century writers take their concept of the high style, and everywhere one looks in the poetry of the latter half of the century one can see the effect of his influence. It is at its most extreme in the semi-liturgical excesses of 'halff chongyd Latyne, with conseytys off poetry/And craffty Imagynacionys off ymagys ffantastyk', as Lydgate's fellow East Anglian poet, John Metham,[9] expressed it, but he is identifiable too in the habit of rhetorical variation and repeated illustration of the same idea. Lydgate's influence on fifteenth-century style can be seen as pernicious, but it has its more positive aspects. Early fifteenth-century poetry is limited in resource. In Hoccleve, for instance, one finds (despite the interest of his autobiographical works) a painfully flat, threadbare poetic vocabulary, gauchely handled. Through Lydgate's greater ambition – long-winded, pretentious and artificial as the results often are – fifteenth-century poetry grew and diversified. And the drama developed its poetic resources along with the narrative poetry of the period.

There is plenty of evidence for the association of other East Anglian writers and aspirations to the high style. It was probably John of Norwich who, early in the century, wrote the *Tractatus de modo inueniendi ornata verba*,[10] and later one can cite the works of John Metham and Osborn Bokenham as showing interest in and command of elaborate rhetorical expression. John Capgrave, Austin Friar of Lynn, is best known for his *Chronicle* but he also wrote 'embellished hagiography' in his lives of St Norbert and St Katherine in rhyme-royal stanzas.[11] The sixteenth-century Norwich Grocers' Play is a particularly extreme example of the East Anglian high style – full of polysyllables and periphrases. More discriminating uses are found within the plays discussed in earlier chapters. The interest in creating a high style came partly from the desire to find a mode of expression suitable for God, but it also developed into the resounding bombast of tyrants, the specious wheedlings of the Devil in disguise, and as a contrast to more colloquial, realistic manners of speech. Elevated expression in *Mankind* has profited from the example of Lydgate and as a result the dramatist shows a more convincing sense of appropriate variation of style than the author of *The Castle of Perseverance*, whose main tools of heightened expression are insistent alliteration and complex stanza forms. There are no great poets among the late medieval dramatists, but there is a growing interest in using the way that things are expressed as part of the range of idea and feeling in the plays. In *Wisdom*, *Magnificence* and elsewhere the poets intelligently vary the metres to fit the characters and the mood of a scene and Skelton shows a skilful command of the use of exaggerated style to indicate an assumed attitude.

The East Anglian plays of the period include the three Macro plays, the manuscript of which stayed in Bury St Edmunds until the eighteenth century, the fragment of the play called *Dux Moraud*, written in the Bury St Edmunds dialect, the Croxton *Play of the Sacrament*, which includes local references to the Thetford and Bury St Edmunds area, and a number of other pageants and fragments which have not hitherto been discussed.[12] Of these, also connected with Bury St Edmunds is the Rickinghall fragment which includes some Anglo-Norman lines, followed by an English rendering of part, from a speech by an assertive king, possibly Herod. Two more fragments survive in the late fifteenth century common-place book compiled by Robert Reynes of Acle; here occurs, first, a sixty line speech in stanzas for a character called Delight, beginning

> Lo, here is a ladde lyght,
> Al fresch I you plyght,
> Galant and jolly . . .

and including such learned words as *redolent, solacious, florent* and *refulsyth*; the second fragment is the Epilogue to a play, 30 lines in two 13-line stanzas plus a quatrain, in an elaborate literary style, again with a significant sprinkling of learned words, such as *eloquensy, incressement, laudabyl*, and *neglygensy*. The Brome *Abraham* from Suffolk and the Norwich Grocers' Play of the Creation of Adam and Eve and the expulsion from Paradise provide evidence of activity in the composition of scriptural drama.[13] If one broadens out into the East Midlands area in general, then, in addition, the N-Town cycle, *Mary Magdalene* and possibly other of the Digby plays may be added to the list. The Digby MS was owned by Miles Blomefylde (physician, born in 1525 at Bury St Edmunds), as was the only known copy of *Fulgens and Lucres*.

In this substantial body of material one can see evidence of very varied dramatic activity. The scope and style of the plays show different degrees of ambition, sophistication and physical and financial resources. Behind the confused and scrappy picture which results from putting all these plays together one can see dimly shaping a pattern in the development of the drama. This pattern is not formed by several distinct kinds of religious drama, each with its own origin, history and type of performance, but by the sporadic but progressive fusion of instructive clerical chronicle-plays, the use of pageants in civic and ecclesiastical ceremonies, and the growth of audiences, in noble and religious houses, in cities, in universities, for imaginative entertainment in dramatic form. The introduction of printing perhaps fed an interest in short topical plays, if Wynkyn de Worde's printing of *Youth, Hick Scorner* and *Mundus et Infans* may be taken as an indicator; these same plays hint also that a type of short play developed from fifteenth-century allegorical poems.[14] In the history of the monarchy and the great barons of the fifteenth century one can see the living material out of which might be bred reflections on the mutability of fortune and the transitoriness of earthly power and possession, as well as the satirical quips of the poor about the rich. Even within the circle known to Lydgate, the character and career of Henry VI, the prosperity and the downfall of Humphrey, Duke of Gloucester, and of his wife, Eleanor, tried for witchcraft in 1441, show the currents of life which lie behind the fifteenth-century moralists' obsession with the sudden twists of fate.

I have tried in this book to suggest the range of English drama in the fifteenth century. Though it is not a period of great playwrights, it is a period in which dramatists are enterprising; some were working with limited talent or with limited means but nevertheless exploring the possibilities of theatrical expression. The modern view of the period will continue to be blurred because of lack of evidence, but that is not an excuse for accepting an over-simplified view of the history of plays in the late medieval period. The range of dramatic kinds, the influence on drama of Lydgate and other contemporary writers of poetry and prose, the importance of universities and powerful ecclesiastics in promoting dramatic activity, the possibilities in East Anglian religious houses for the satisfaction of a taste for lavish display and grandiose language, all these are important threads which go to make up our still incomplete picture. The explanation of the nature of medieval plays has often been far too narrow and too sure, as in the simple classification of plays as offshoots of medieval preaching. Whereas the preachers are concerned with moral warnings, the dramatists and poets are concerned with illustration. The plays of the late medieval period exploit and extend the different forms and types of illustration available: the tragic picture of the reversal of fortune, the comic sequence of the acquisition of wisdom, the symbolic tableau of moral states, corrupt and pure, and the episodic panorama of man's life on earth, his history, his journey and his reward.

Notes

Names in capitals are abbreviated forms of authors and titles which will be found in full in the bibliography.

I. *Genres*

1. Successive versions of the history of medieval drama may be found in E. K. Chambers, *The Medieval Stage* (2 vols) (Oxford, 1903); Karl Young, *The Drama of the Medieval Church* (2 vols) (Oxford, 1933); Hardin Craig, *English Religious Drama of the Middle Ages* (Oxford, 1955); O. B. Hardison, Jr., *Christian Rite and Christian Drama in the Middle Ages* (Baltimore, 1965); R. Axton, *European Drama of the Early Middle Ages* (London, 1974). On the English plays see KOLVE; E. Prosser, *Drama and Religion in the English Mystery Plays* (Stanford, 1961); WOOLF; KAHRL. The most recent contributions are WICKHAM 3 and REVELS. Wickham adheres to the idea that 'there is some justification for the long-established critical belief that the English cycles of miracle plays are best accounted for in terms of some evolutionary process' but goes on to emphasise 'the no less important break with tradition represented in the switch of doctrinal emphasis within the new drama away from Christ's divinity and towards his humanity; away from a primary concern with establishment of faith and towards a no less urgent concern with repentance.' WICKHAM 3, p. 41.
2. See Richard Southern, *The Medieval Theatre in the Round* (London, 1957), WICKHAM 1, TYDEMAN.
3. See WICKHAM 3, Book One 'Drama and Occasion' on recurrent and non-recurrent festivals.
4. The N-Town cycle is a composite cycle in which have been joined together some plays written for movable wagons, a group of plays about the life of the Virgin which have been adapted for a single location, and the central Passion Plays written for fixed place-and-scaffold. It used to be thought the cycle of Coventry, and since that idea has been discredited has been attributed to Lincoln and Norwich. Nowadays it is identified from the Banns which speak of beginning the performance on 'Sunday next . . . / At vj of the belle . . . / In N. towne.' If N stands for Latin *nomen*, 'name', then it might indicate that the cycle was taken on tour and the name of the local town inserted at this point. See Hardin Craig, *English Religious Drama of the Middle Ages* (Oxford, 1955); he prefers yet a third name for the cycle, the Hegge Plays. See also WOOLF, KAHRL, pp. 59–69 on the staging of the Passion Play.
5. *The Pride of Life, Dux Moraud, The Play of the Sacrament* are in DAVIS. *The Castle of Perseverance, Mankind* and *Wisdom* are in ECCLES. *Youth* and *Hick Scorner* appear as *Two Tudor Interludes*, ed. Ian Lancashire (Manchester, 1980). *Youth* and *Mundus et Infans* are in E. T. Schell and J. D. Schuchter, *English Morality Plays and Moral Interludes* (New York, 1969). *Youth* and *The Pride of Life* are in HAPPÉ TI. *Mankind* and *Fulgens and Lucres* are in *English Moral Interludes* ed. G. Wickham (London, 1976). *The Castle of Perseverance* and *Magnificence* are in *Four Morality Plays*, ed. P. Happé (Harmondsworth, 1979). Other useful anthologies are J. A. B. Somerset, *Four Tudor Interludes* (London, 1974) and D. M. Bevington, *Medieval Drama* (Boston, 1975). For editions of individual cycles, plays of known authorship, etc., see bibliography.

6. See Chapter VI below for further comment on the importance of East Anglia.
7. See KOLVE for fuller discussion of typology in the cycles.
8. A recent example is Derek Pearsall, *Old English and Middle English Poetry* (London, 1977), p. 252.
9. C. S. Lewis, *English Literature in the Sixteenth Century excluding Drama* (Oxford, 1954). E. K. Chambers, *English Literature at the Close of the Middle Ages* (Oxford, 1945). H. S. Bennett, *Chaucer and the Fifteenth Century* (Oxford, 1947).
10. Editors' note in *English Literature at the Close of the Middle Ages*.
11. OWST, p. 473.
12. OWST, p. 475.
13. Allardyce Nicoll, *British Drama* (London, 1925), p. 23, quoted by OWST, p. 475.
14. WOOLF, pp. 179–80, 193–4, etc.
15. W. A. Davenport, *The Art of the Gawain-Poet* (London, 1978) where I suggest the dramatic Herods as origins for Belshazzar, etc. It now seems to me as likely to be the other way round.
16. *The Awntyrs off Arthure at the Terne Wathelyn*, ed. Ralph Hanna III (Manchester, 1974).

II. *Pride, Death and Tragedy*

1. See the account in DAVIS, pp. lxxxv–lxxxviii.
2. Carleton Brown, 'The *Pride of Life* and the "Twelve Abuses"', *Archiv* 127 (1912), 72–8.
3. *Death and Liffe*, ed. Sir I. Gollancz (London, 1930).
4. See TRISTRAM, esp. pp. 34–48.
5. See POTTER, p. 14.
6. The most striking is in Chaucer's *The Book of the Duchess* where death is symbolised by Fortune's taking of the Queen. The word for Queen is *fers*, which punningly links with *fiers*, 'bold', 'proud'. The modern rooks or castles appeared as foot-soldiers in the famous medieval set from Lewis, though it is more usual in European sets for pawns to represent infantry.
7. Boethius, *De Consolatione Philosophiae* as translated by Chaucer, Book II, prose 2.
8. ibid.
9. *The Canterbury Tales*, VII, 2771–3.
10. FARNHAM, p. 168.
11. Text cited is from *English Verse between Chaucer and Surrey*, ed. E. P. Hammond (Durham, N. Carolina, 1927). See also *The Dance of Death*, ed. F. Warren and B. White, EETS os 181 (London, 1931).
12. See TRISTRAM, pp. 36–7.
13. *Religious Lyrics of the XIVth Century*, ed. Carleton Brown (Oxford, 1924), poem 101, p. 143.
14. FARNHAM, p. 175. See also WICKHAM 3: 'tragi-comedy was the basic or natural dramatic form for English play-makers of the Middle Ages.' (p. 178).
15. A different view is that true tragedy did not develop until later: eg. J. M. R. Margeson, *The Origins of English Tragedy* (London, 1967) says, 'When the nature and the intensity of the human experience became a matter of greater concern in the drama than the moral idea, then tragedy became possible.' (pp. 58–9). See WICKHAM 3, pp. 220 ff. and 251–2.
16. Paula Neuss puts the emphasis differently: 'The repentance and renewal of Magnificence show finally that the play is a moral one, not a true tragedy of a prince's fall, yet the choice of a prince for hero, and the placing of that prince in a "historical" setting with a life of his own, makes for something, if only

potentially, similar to medieval tragedy.' [John Skelton, *Magnificence*, ed. Paula Neuss (Manchester, 1980), p. 22.] Lois Potter's discussion in REVELS, pp. 173–6, does not get as far.

17. POTTER, p. 53.
18. A. C. Cawley in his edition of *Everyman*, p. xxiii.
19. David J. Leigh, 'The Doomsday Mystery Play: An Eschatological Morality', *Modern Philology* 67 (1969–70), 211–23, reprinted in TAYLOR and NELSON.

III. *Mankind and Medieval Comedy*

1. E. K. Chambers, *English Literature at the Close of the Middle Ages* (Oxford, 1945), pp. 61 and 62.
2. W. K. Smart, 'Some Notes on *Mankind*', *Modern Philology* 14 (1916–17), p. 120. A. W. Pollard, *English Miracle Plays, Moralities and Interludes* (8th edition, Oxford, 1927), p. xlix.
3. Sister M. P. Coogan, *An Interpretation of the Moral Play Mankind* (Washington, 1947).
4. Coogan, p. 89.
5. See Paula Neuss, 'Active and Idle Language: Dramatic Images in *Mankind*', in DENNY, 40–67; Kathleen M. Ashley, 'Titivillus and the Battle of Words in *Mankind*', *Annuale Mediaevale* 16 (1975), 128–50; Lorraine K. Stock, 'The Thematic and Structural Unity of *Mankind*', *Studies in Philology* 72 (1975), 386–407.
6. e.g. a very successful production by Robert Gordon at Royal Holloway College (University of London) in 1979.
7. B. Spivack, *Shakespeare and the Allegory of Evil* (New York and London, 1958), p. 123.
8. Robert A. Potter, *The Form and Concept of the English Morality Play* (dissertation, Claremont 1963), p. 190 (quoted in KAHRL, p. 105). Potter seems to have left this out of *The English Morality Play*.
9. Merle Fifield, *The Rhetoric of Free Will: the Five-action Structure of the English Morality Play* (Leeds, 1974).
10. John Conley, '"Reson" in *Mankind* 173', *Notes and Queries* 23 (October 1976), 447–8, points out that 'reson' is synonymous with 'acownte' in l. 177.
11. or, as Southern suggests, from concealment behind screens in a hall. SOUTHERN, p. 143.
12. *Jacob's Well*, ed. A. Brandeis, EETS os 115 (London, 1890), Chapter 37. See also Chapter 50. WICKHAM 3, pp. 131–3, connects the spade symbol in the two texts.
13. See Coogan, p. 59.
14. This is not quite what is meant by Michael Kelley by his term 'flamboyant drama', but he draws attention to the 'ornamental mixture of detailed realistic description with those rhetorical devices associated with the high style . . .'. *Flamboyant Drama* (Carbondale and Edwardsville, Southern Illinois, 1979), p. 17.
15. *The Pardoner's Prologue*, 435–8, quoted by OWST, p. 153.
16. See G. R. Owst, *Preaching in Medieval England* (Cambridge, 1926), p. 299 ff. The standard work on exempla is J. A. Mosher, *The Exemplum in the early Religious and Didactic Literature of England* (New York, 1911).
17. The comparison between Gower and Chaucer tends to favour Chaucer rather too easily. As with Richardson (in comparison with Fielding), so with Gower: moment-by-moment representation requires length.
18. In the tales of the Physician and Manciple, for instance.

19. Chaucer treats Elde also in the Reeve's Prologue; the longing for release and the relentless refusal of Death 'to closen wepynge eien' has its source in Boethius, Bk I, metrum 1.
20. *Jacob's Well*, ed. A. Brandeis, p. vi.
21. ibid., p. 105, ll. 23–35.
22. ibid., p. 114, ll. 26–30.
23. ibid., p. 237, ll. 14–21.
24. Siegfried Wenzel, *The Sin of Sloth: Acedia in Medieval Thought and Literature* (Chapel Hill, N. Carolina, 1967), pp. 150–55.
25. *Le Roman de la Rose* in particular.
26. Robert of Brunne's *Handlyng Synne*, ed. F. J. Furnivall, EETS os 119 (London 1901).
27. Peter Idley's *Instructions to his Son*, ed. Charlotte d'Evelyn, Modern Language Association of America Monograph Series VI (Boston and London, 1935).
28. Idley, Bk IIB, 946–52.
29. Idley, Bk IIB, 1170–71.
30. See Woolf, pp. 174–7.
31. In Davis.
32. See Heuser in *Anglia* XXX, 201–5; Davis, pp. ciii–cv.
33. The version with an innocent heroine is better-known, as in *Emaré*, ed. E. Rickert, EETS os 99 (London, 1908).
34. With some honourable exceptions: see Owst, Chaps. V–VII and Peter.
35. Jill Mann, *Chaucer and Medieval Estates Satire: the Literature of Social Classes and the General Prologue to the Canterbury Tales* (Cambridge, 1973).
36. *The Parson's Tale*, 421–3.
37. See Owst, especially Chapter V, for a full illustration.
38. See V. J. Scattergood, *Politics and Poetry in the Fifteenth Century* (London, 1971), Chapters 8–10.
39. *Historical Poems of the XIVth and XVth Centuries*, ed. R. H. Robbins (New York, 1959), p. 127.
40. *Historical Poems*, pp. 138–9. See also the *Treatyse of a Gallant*, ed. F. J. Furnivall, *Ballads from Manuscripts* (2 vols., 1868–72), I 445–53, in which the vanity of absurd fashions is linked to the Seven Deadly Sins by an acrostic on the letters of Galawnt: this yields gluttony, avarice/arrogance, lechery, accidie and wrath/vanity easily, but the poet has to resort to niceness (folly)/negligence and treachery/tyranny to make up his set. See M. W. Bloomfield, *The Seven Deadly Sins* (Michigan, 1952), pp. 206–7.
41. Peter, p. 9.
42. Peter, p. 47.
43. See, for instance, N. Denny, 'Aspects of the Staging of *Mankind*', *Medium Aevum* 43, 1974, 252–63.
44. References are respectively to: L. W. Cushman, *The Devil and the Vice in the English Dramatic Literature before Shakespeare* (Studien zur englischen Philologie 6, Halle, 1900); D. M. Bevington, *From Mankind to Marlowe* (Cambridge, Mass., 1962); S. Wenzel, *The Sin of Sloth* (Chapel Hill, N. Carolina 1967); L. K. Stock, 'The Thematic and Structural Unity of *Mankind*', *Studies in Philology* 72 (1975), 386–407.
45. Southern, p. 143.
46. Peter, p. 68.
47. Woolf, p. 131.
48. *Two Tudor Interludes*, ed. Ian Lancashire (The Revels Plays, Manchester 1980), pp. 15–71.
49. Cf. the use of the same imagery in *Mankind*.
50. Lancashire, p. 59.
51. In Davis.

52. DAVIS, pp. lxxxiv–v.
53. Sister Nicholas Maltman in 'Meaning and Art in the Croxton *Play of the Sacrament*', *English Literary History* 41 (1974), 149–64, claims that the play 'is comedy only in so far as it ends happily. The impulse behind the play was pastoral and didactic, the message of the play is doctrinal, its matrix liturgical and its tone serious.' (p. 162) and that the humour works by ironic contrast (e.g. between the comic doctor and Christ, the true physician). She has a point, and the play ends seriously, but it is not merely that some scenes will strike 'the modern reader as crude and grotesque'; they *are* crude and grotesque and I cannot believe that they would not have seemed so when first performed.
54. *The Plays of Henry Medwall*, ed. Alan H. Nelson (Cambridge, 1980). Also in *English Moral Interludes*, ed. G. Wickham (London, 1976). See SOUTHERN, pp. 95–126.
55. Anne Righter, *Shakespeare and the Idea of the Play* (London, 1964), p. 37. See also Lois Potter in REVELS, pp. 162–4.

IV.   *Wisdom and the Drama of Ideas*

1. See ECCLES.
2. See W. K. Smart, *Some English and Latin Sources and Parallels for the Morality of Wisdom* (Menasha, Wisconsin, 1912). More recently, Milton McC. Gatch, 'Mysticism and Satire in the Morality of *Wisdom*', *Philological Quarterly* 53 (1974), 342–62.
3. ECCLES, p. xxxvi. C. G. Tucker Brooke, *The Tudor Drama* (1911) was also being disparaging when he said, 'The piece is indeed more masque or ballet than drama.', but I would, without any disparagement, agree with his description.
4. See Michael Kelley, *Flamboyant Drama* (Carbondale and Edwardsville, Southern Illinois, 1979), Chapter 4.
5. WICKHAM 3, pp. 110–11, describes these as mummings. A. R. Heiserman, *Skelton and Satire* (Chicago 1961) discusses their satirical characteristics in his chapter on *Magnificence*.
6. 'Subtleties' were table decorations of holy scenes or symbolic devices made from sugar or pastry and brought in between courses. Lydgate designed some of these (as well as tableaux). See WICKHAM 1, pp. 211 ff.
7. For more about Lydgate's Mummings see Section 3 of this chapter.
8. See Smart, op. cit., pp. 34–7.
9. A suggestion made by J. J. Molloy in *A Theological Interpretation of the Moral Play Wisdom Who is Christ* (Washington, 1952); Chambers suggested schoolboys, Smart monks. Gatch (in the article cited in Note 2 above) argues for connection with the London household of the Bishop of Ely, in the vicinity of the Inns of Court. William Grey, Bishop of Ely 1454–78, was a patron of learning with humanist leanings. His successor was John Morton (Bishop 1479–86), later patron of Henry Medwall.
10. I find the academic/devotional background a more convincing explanation of the nature of *Wisdom* than suggestions of political allegory, such as were made by R. L. Ramsay in his edition of Skelton's *Magnyfycence*, EETS es xcviii (London, 1908), p. lxxi, and more recently by D. M. Bevington, *Tudor Drama and Politics* (Cambridge, Mass., 1968), pp. 29–34.
11. Thomas Chaundler, *Liber Apologeticus de Omni Statu Humanae Naturae*, ed. Doris Enright-Clark-Shoukri (The Modern Humanities Research Association, London and New York, 1974). The quotation is from p. 12.

12. See R. Weiss, *Humanism in England during the Fifteenth Century* (Oxford, 1941), pp. 133–6.
13. CHAUNDLER, p. 15.
14. ibid. p. 82. The translation is mine.
15. ibid. p. 94.
16. ibid. p. 150.
17. ibid. p. 158.
18. ibid. p. 12.
19. ibid. p. 22.
20. See WOOLF, pp. 164–9 on this play.
21. See D. A. Pearsall, *Old English and Middle English Poetry* (London, 1977), pp. 242–3.
22. Hope Traver, *The Four Daughters of God* (Philadelphia, 1907), pp. 125–40. See also ECCLES, note on p. 200.
23. There are accounts in several places. See, for instance, TYDEMAN, pp. 77–8 and a fuller account in WICKHAM 1, pp. 208–10. The evidence is an eye-witness account in College of Arms MS. 1st M13. On Masque see Enid Welsford, *The Court Masque* (Cambridge, 1927).
24. See WOOLF, p. 98, and *English Gilds, their Statues and Customs A.D. 1389*, ed. Toulmin Smith and Lucy Toulmin Smith, EETS os 40 (London, 1870), p. 149. Also TYDEMAN, p. 96.
25. W. F. Schirmer, *John Lydgate, A Study in the Culture of the XVth Century* [translated A. E. Keep from the German original published 1952] (London, 1961), p. 104. D. A. Pearsall, *John Lydgate* (London, 1970), p. 183. *The Pageant of Knowledge* is in *The Minor Poems of John Lydgate*, Vol. II, pp. 724–38.
26. WICKHAM 1, pp. 191 ff., Schirmer, Chap. 13, Pearsall *John Lydgate* pp. 183–8. WICKHAM 3, pp. 48–52 and (on the *Mumming at Hertford*) pp. 194–5.
27. See WOOLF, p. 399, note 15. Dieter Mehl, *The Elizabethan Dumb-Show* (London, 1965).

V.   *The Castle of Perseverance and the Long Play*

1. See especially Richard Southern, *The Medieval Theatre in the Round: A study of the Staging of The Castle of Perseverance and Related Matters* (London, 1957), and N. C. Schmitt, 'Was there a Medieval Theatre in the Round?', *Theatre Notebook* 23 (1969), 1–13, reprinted in TAYLOR and NELSON, pp. 292–315. See for a summary TYDEMAN, pp. 156–9.
2. A good summary of *Psychomachia* is in Bernard Spivack, *Shakespeare and the Allegory of Evil* (New York and London, 1958).
3. See ECCLES, p. xx and p. 186 on the sources of the play and the author's possible use of *Le Chasteau d'Amour* of Robert Grosseteste.
4. Edgar T. Schell, 'On the Imitation of Life's Pilgrimage in *The Castle of Perseverance*', *Journal of English and Germanic Philology* 67 (1968), 235–48, reprinted in TAYLOR and NELSON, pp. 279–91.
5. This is the pattern used by ECCLES; Peter Happé in *Four Morality Plays* (Harmondsworth, 1979) prefers a division into four sections to correspond to the allegorical structure: First Temptation, Second Temptation, Death, Mercy.
6. On Trevisa see D. C. Fowler, *The Bible in Early English Literature* (London, 1977), Chapter 6 and pp. 253–4.
7. M. C. Seymour et al. (edd.), *On the Properties of Things: John Trevisa's Translation of Bartolomaeus Anglicus De Proprietatibus Rerum* (2 vols: London, 1975), Vol. I, p. 293.

8. ibid.
9. For a specific resemblance see A. Nelson, '*Of the Seven Ages*: an unknown analogue of *The Castle of Perseverance*', *Comparative Drama* 8 (1974), 125–38.
10. *Complete Works of John Gower*, ed. G. C. Macaulay (4 volumes, Oxford, 1899–1902).
11. *The Court of Sapience*, ed. R. Spindler (Leipzig, 1927). Extracts from the poem may be found in *English Verse between Chaucer and Surrey*, ed. E. P. Hammond (Durham, N. Carolina, 1927).
12. Stephen Hawes, *The Pastime of Pleasure* ed. W. E. Mead, EETS os 173 (London, 1928).
13. See TRISTRAM, pp. 77–94.
14. In *Hymns to the Virgin and Christ* . . . ed. F. J. Furnivall, EETS os 24 (London, 1867), pp. 58–78.
15. See discussion of the play in KAHRL, pp. 106–14 and WICKHAM 3, pp. 163–5.
16. See SOUTHERN, pp. 126–142.
17. WOOLF, p. 312. See also D. L. Jeffrey, 'English Saints' Plays', in DENNY, 69–90.
18. On *Nature* see *The Plays of Henry Medwall* ed. Alan H. Nelson (Cambridge, 1980), SOUTHERN, pp. 55–94, POTTER, especially pp. 58–66, and REVELS, pp. 165–6.
19. Nelson takes a more charitable view: 'We may rest well pleased with what Medwall offers in his two plays: vitality of language, metrical felicity, liveliness of characterisation, intriguing descriptions of London life, amusing situations, good jokes, practical tricks, supplementary entertainment, and excellent good sense.' *The Plays of Henry Medwall*, p. 28.

VI. *Scope and Style: Lydgate and East Anglian Drama*

1. Particularly in the works listed in the Bibliography by SOUTHERN, WICKHAM, in the Revels History and Ian Lancashire's work on the Interludes.
2. D. M. Bevington, *From Mankind to Marlowe* (Cambridge, Mass., 1962), p. 17.
3. SOUTHERN, pp. 21–55, 143–5. ECCLES, p. xlii, considers the idea of an inn.
4. See L. M. Clopper, '*Mankind* and its Audience', *Comparative Drama* 8 (1974–5), 347–55.
5. See R. Axton, *European Drama of the Early Middle Ages* (London, 1974), p. 201.
6. See Schirmer's and Pearsall's books on Lydgate for fuller accounts of the visit.
7. Lydgate, *Minor Poems* Vol. II, pp. 630–48.
8. Edited by Carleton Brown in *MLR* 7 (1912), 225–34.
9. John Metham, *Amoryus and Cleopes* in Metham's *Works*, ed. Hardin Craig, EETS os 132 (London, 1916), p. 80.
10. See R. Weiss, *Humanism in England during the Fifteenth Century*, p. 11.
11. D. Pearsall, *Old English and Middle English Poetry*, p. 252.
12. Note also the record in 1389 of an interludium associated with the guild of Corpus Christi at Bury St Edmunds. See Karl Young, 'An *Interludium* for a Gild of Corpus Christi' *MLN* XLVIII (1933), 84–6. See KOLVE, p. 47. See also N. Davis, 'Two Unprinted Dialogues in Late Middle English and their Language', *Revue des Langues Vivantes* 35 (1969), 461–72, concerning two interludes, possibly East Anglian, *Occupation and Idleness* and *Lucidus and Dubius*.
13. The Rickinghall fragment, the Reynes extracts, the Brome play and the Norwich Grocers' Play are in DAVIS.
14. See Ian Lancashire, 'The Sources of *Hyckescorner*', *Review of English Studies* ns 22 (1971), 257–73.

Bibliography

Works cited in the notes or in the text in an abbreviated form are here identified first by the abbreviation in CAPITALS. I have not listed here all the works referred to in the text, since there seemed no need to duplicate all the information in the notes.

Editions of Plays
D. M. Bevington, *Medieval Drama* (Boston, 1975)
CHESTER *The Chester Mystery Cycle*, ed. R. M. Lumiansky and David Mills, EETS ss 3 (London, 1974).
CHAUNDLER Thomas Chaundler, *Liber Apologeticus de omni statu humanae naturae*, ed. D. Enright-Clark-Shoukri (London and New York, 1974).
DAVIS N. Davis (ed.), *Non-Cycle Plays and Fragments*, EETS ss 1 (London, 1970).
The Digby Plays, ed. F. J. Furnivall, EETS es LXX (London, 1896).
ECCLES M. Eccles (ed.), *The Macro Plays*, EETS 262 (London, 1969).
Everyman, ed. A. C. Cawley (Manchester, 1961).
J. S. Farmer, *Six Anonymous Plays*, first series 1510–37 (London, 1905) [contains *Everyman*, *Hickscorner*, *Mundus et Infans*].
J. S. Farmer, *'Lost' Tudor Plays* (London, 1907) [contains *Mankind*, *Nature*].
HAPPÉ TI P. Happé (ed.), *Tudor Interludes* (Harmondsworth, 1972) [contains *The Pride of Life*, extracts from *Mankind* and from *Fulgens and Lucres*, *Youth*].
P. Happé (ed.), *English Mystery Plays* (Harmondsworth, 1975).
P. Happé (ed.), *Four Morality Plays* (Harmondsworth, 1979).
Ian Lancashire (ed.), *Two Tudor Interludes* (Manchester, 1980).
J. M. Manly, *Specimens of the Pre-Shaksperean Drama*, Vol. 1 (London, 1897).
Alan H. Nelson (ed.), *The Plays of Henry Medwall* (Cambridge, 1980).
N-TOWN *Ludus Coventriae*, ed. K. S. Block, EETS es CXX (London, 1922).
E. T. Schell and J. D. Schuchter, *English Morality Plays and Moral Interludes* (New York, 1969).
John Skelton, *Magnyfycence*, ed. R. L. Ramsay, EETS es XCVIII (London, 1908).
John Skelton, *Magnificence*, ed. P. Neuss (Manchester, 1980).
J. A. B. Somerset, *Four Tudor Interludes* (London, 1974).
TOWNELEY *The Towneley Plays*, ed. G. England and A. W. Pollard, EETS es LXXI (London, 1897).
The Wakefield Pageants in the Towneley Cycle, ed. A. C. Cawley (Manchester, 1958).
G. Wickham, *English Moral Interludes* (London, 1976).
YORK *York Plays*, ed. L. Toulmin Smith (Oxford, 1885).

Other Medieval Texts
Geoffrey Chaucer, *The Works of . . .* , ed. F. N. Robinson (2nd edn, Boston and London, 1957).
E. P. Hammond, *English Verse between Chaucer and Surrey* (Durham, N. Carolina, 1927).
Robert of Brunne's *Handlyng Synne*, ed. F. J. Furnivall, EETS os 119 (London, 1901).
Hymns to the Virgin and Christ, ed. F. J. Furnivall, EETS os 24 (London, 1867) [contains 'The Mirror of the Periods of Man's Life'].
Peter Idley's *Instructions to his Son*, ed. C. d'Evelyn (Boston and London, 1935).
Jacob's Well, ed. A. Brandeis, EETS os 115 (London, 1900).
William Langland, *The Vision of Piers Plowman*, the B-Text, ed. A. V. C. Schmidt (London, 1978).

John Lydgate, *The Pilgrimage of the Life of Man*, ed. F. J. Furnivall, Part I, EETS es LXXVII (London, 1899), Part II, EETS es LXXXIII (London, 1901).

John Lydgate, *The Fall of Princes*, ed. H. Bergen, EETS es CXXI-CXXIV (London, 1924–7).

John Lydgate, *Minor Poems*, ed. H. N. MacCracken, Part I, EETS es CVII (London, 1911), Part II, EETS os 192 (London, 1934).

The Works of Sir Thomas Malory, ed. E. Vinaver, 3 vols., (2nd edn., London, 1967).

The Parlement of the Thre Ages, ed. M. Y. Offord, EETS 246 (London, 1959).

The Book of Vices and Virtues, ed. W. N. Francis, EETS 217 (London, 1942).

Wynnere and Wastoure, ed. I. Gollancz (London, 1920).

History and Criticism

R. Axton, *European Drama of the Early Middle Ages* (London, 1974).

D. M. Bevington, *From Mankind to Marlowe* (Cambridge, Mass., 1962).

M. W. Bloomfield, *The Seven Deadly Sins* (Michigan, 1952).

E. K. Chambers, *The Medieval Stage*, 2 vols. (Oxford, 1903).

G. Clifford, *The Transformations of Allegory* (London and Boston, 1974).

COOGAN M. P. Coogan, *An Interpretation of the Moral Play 'Mankind'* (Washington, 1947).

H. Craig, *English Religious Drama of the Middle Ages* (Oxford, 1955).

DENNY N. Denny (ed.), *Medieval Drama*, Stratford-upon-Avon Studies 16 (London, 1973).

FARNHAM W. Farnham, *The Medieval Heritage of Elizabethan Tragedy* (Berkeley, California, 1936).

S. D. Feldman, *The Morality-Patterned Comedy of the Renaissance* (The Hague, 1970).

A. Fletcher, *Allegory: the Theory of a Symbolic Mode* (New York, 1964).

P. O. E. Gradon, *Form and Style in Early English Literature* (London, 1971).

O. B. Hardison, Jr., *Christian Rite and Christian Drama in the Middle Ages* (Baltimore, 1965).

KAHRL S. J. Kahrl, *Traditions of Medieval English Drama* (London, 1974).

M. R. Kelley, *Flamboyant Drama: a Study of 'The Castle of Perseverance', 'Mankind' and 'Wisdom'* (Carbondale and Edwardsville, Southern Illinois, 1979).

KOLVE V. A. Kolve, *The Play called Corpus Christi* (Stanford, 1966).

W. R. Mackenzie, *The English Moralities from the Point of View of Allegory* (New York, 1914).

G. R. Owst, *Preaching in Medieval England* (Cambridge, 1926).

OWST G. R. Owst, *Literature and Pulpit in Medieval England* (Cambridge, 1933).

D. A. Pearsall, *John Lydgate* (London, 1970).

D. A. Pearsall, *Old English and Middle English Poetry* (London, 1977).

PETER J. Peter, *Complaint and Satire in Early English Literature* (Oxford, 1956).

POTTER R. Potter, *The English Morality Play* (London and Boston, 1975).

E. Prosser, *Drama and Religion in the English Mystery Plays* (Stanford, 1961).

REVELS *The Revels History of Drama in English*, Vol. II 1500–1576 (London and New York, 1980).

V. J. Scattergood, *Politics and Poetry in the Fifteenth Century* (London, 1971).

W. F. Schirmer, *John Lydgate: a Study in the Culture of the XVth Century*, translated by A. E. Keep (London, 1961).

R. Southern, *The Medieval Theatre in the Round* (London, 1957).

SOUTHERN R. Southern, *The Staging of Plays before Shakespeare* (London, 1973).

TAYLOR and NELSON J. Taylor and A. H. Nelson (edd.), *Medieval English Drama* (Chicago and London, 1972).

TRISTRAM P. Tristram, *Figures of Life and Death in Medieval English Literature* (London, 1976).

R. Tuve, *Allegorical Imagery* (Princeton, N.J., 1966).

TYDEMAN W. Tydeman, *The Theatre in the Middle Ages* (Cambridge, 1978).

R. Weiss, *Humanism in England during the Fifteenth Century* (Oxford, 1941).

WICKHAM 1   Glynne Wickham, *Early English Stages, Vol. 1 1300–1576* (London, 1959).

WICKHAM 3   Glynne Wickham, *Early English Stages 1300–1660* Vol. 3: Plays and Their Makers to 1576 (London and Henley, 1981).

WOOLF   R. Woolf, *The English Mystery Plays* (London, 1972).

K. Young, *The Drama of the Medieval Church* (2 vols., Oxford, 1933).

INDEX

Abuses of the Age 12, 16, 56, 63–5, 67–8, 71, 87
Accidie, see Sins
Adam 5, 7, 18, 26, 43, 66, 98
Age 12, 50, 110, 115–9, 126
Ages of Man, 19, 110, 114–8, 127
allegory 7–8, 13, 17–8, 20, 31, 44, 48, 50, 58, 63, 71, 77, 87–9, 91, 99, 103, 111–2, 117, 121–3, 126, 128, 130, 134, 136
alliteration 10, 61, 76, 106, 110, 130, 135
Ancrene Wisse 9, 59, 80
Annas 7, 59, 104
Aristotle 32, 81
Athelston 60
Augustine 96, 115
aureate style 10, 30, 37–40, 46–8, 75, 79, 121, 135–6
Ausonius 102, 103
Awntyrs of Arthur, The 14
Axton, R. 132
Ayenbite of Inwit 51

Barclay, Alexander 66, 68
Bartholomaeus Anglicus 115
Bernard of Cluny 64
Bernard, St 96, 99
Beverley 71, 102
Blomefylde, Miles 136
Boccaccio 21–2
Boethius 20–1, 96, 114, 127
Bokenham, Osborn 135
Bonaventura 95, 99
Boy, see *Garcio*
Brandon, Charles, Duke of Suffolk 71
Brome Play of Abraham 136
Bromyard, John 49
Bury St Edmunds 3, 60, 75, 132, 134, 136

Caiaphas 7, 59
Cain 5, 7, 69–71
Cambridge 45, 89, 132, 134
Capgrave, John 135
Castle of Perseverance, The 2, 4, 10, 19, 36, 61, 79, 96, 99–101, 106–114, 116–20, 125–8, 135
Chambers, E. K. 11, 36
Charter of the Abbey of the Holy Ghost, The 96
Chaucer, Alice 134
Chaucer, Geoffrey 20–2, 49–51, 60, 62, 69, 77, 104, 114, 117, 127, 131
   The Astrolabe 114
   The Canterbury Tales 50, 62, 128
      The General Prologue 62–3
      The Man of Law's Tale 60
      The Monk's Tale 21

      The Pardoner's Tale 50–1, 67, 117
      The Parson's Tale 51, 62–3
   The Parliament of Fowls 13
   Troilus and Criseyde 21, 27–8, 127
Chaucer, Thomas 134
Chaundler, Thomas 2, 92–6, 100
   Liber Apologeticus 2, 43, 99–101
Chester Cycle 2, 3, 10, 12, 24–5, 34–5, 66, 97, 129
Christ 1, 4–10, 12–13, 19, 27, 40–1, 54–6, 59, 79, 80, 85, 90, 97–101, 110, 122, 124, 127
Christ and the Doctors 97–8
Christ's Burial and Resurrection 2, 10
comedy 4, 29, 36–7, 42, 44–5, 49, 53, 55–7, 62, 66, 69–78, 87, 123, 126, 131
Complaint 16, 56, 63–5, 67–8, 72–3
Contemplacio 9, 98, 101
Conversion of St Paul, The 2, 23, 79
Coogan, Sister M. P. 36, 51
costume, see dress
Court of Sapience, The 99, 117
Covetousness, see Sins
Croxton, see Sacrament
Cursor Mundi 99
Curteys, William 132–3
cycles (see also Chester, N-Town, Towneley, York) 1–11, 23, 27, 64–5, 97, 104–5, 127–9

dance 82–4, 87–9, 91–2, 101–2, 110
Daughters of God, debate of 4, 7, 93–6, 98–101, 107, 113, 117, 128, 134
De Anima 96
Death 4, 9, 15, 17–20, 23–6, 28, 31–5, 50, 65, 94–5, 110, 113, 116–8
Death and Life 13, 18–19, 28
Death of Herod (N-Town) 9, 25–6, 32, 34
debate 12–13, 18, 29, 84, 92–101
Debate between the Soul and Body, The 13
De Casibus Illustrium Virorum, see Boccaccio
Deguileville 112, 117
demons/devils 4, 7, 23, 25, 51–3, 56, 65, 68–9, 89, 122–4
Devil 4–5, 7, 9, 19, 23, 26–7, 43–4, 48, 52, 56, 59, 65–6, 69, 74, 84–6, 88, 93–4, 97, 104–11, 114, 116, 121–2, 124–5, 128, 135
Digby Plays 2, 23, 60, 79, 120, 126–7, 136
disguise 56, 84, 102
'Doctor' 8, 33–4, 98
dress 38–9, 45, 56, 62–3, 66–7, 80– 1, 83–4, 86, 87–92, 102, 104
dumb-show 103–5
Dux Moraud 2, 60–1, 136